C O N T E N T S

Acknowledgments

Introduction   1

I

The Way Things Were   11

II

Into the Locked Bookcase   51

III

Myth-making at Work   73

IV

The Stages of the Myth   105

V

Kafka and Felice: Nothing to Do with Sex 145

VI

Kafka and Milena: All About Sex 183

VII

Why the Myth Must Go 203

Conclusion:
An End and a Beginning 221

Notes *233*

Further Reading *237*

Index *239*

ACKNOWLEDGMENTS

Thanks to . . .

Professor Ritchie Robertson, St. John's College, Oxford, who early on encouraged me to think that I had something worth saying and whose inexplicably generous help later saved me from many solecisms (those that remain are, of course, entirely my own).

Professor Martin Swales, UCL, who kindly commissioned me to write a students' guide to Kafka's novels many years ago: I never did, and hope this is some belated fulfilment of his trust.

The Creative Wales scheme of the Arts Council of Wales, whose substantial financial support let me write this without bringing the bailiffs to my family's door; Andrew Davies and Professor Peter Stead for help in obtaining that support.

Andrew Davies again, for the astounding offer he made when things utterly unrelated to writing had undermined my morale. I was sadly unable to take him up, but the mere thought of such extraordinary generosity was a mighty tonic at a bad time.

Professor Peter-André Alt, Free University of Berlin, Kafka's greatest biographer, who was ready to correspond with and advise on a vital point a non-colleague entirely unknown to him.

My great friends Dr. Peter Thompson (Sheffield) and Dr. Karen Leeder (New College, Oxford) for all the chats, visits, and insights.

My partner, Nerys Lloyd, who put her own career on hold to look after our three sons while I wrote this.

My agent, Stephanie Cabot, who gave me the lunch at which we thought of this book and my editors, Daniela Rapp at St. Martin's Press and Richard Milbank at Quercus, who spotted many errors, great and small.

My mother, who introduced me to the *Prager Tagblatt* many years ago and gave me the story about Arthur Schnitzler's father.

Thanks are also due to the Austrian National Library for the images from the *Prager Tagblatt* that appear on the opening pages of chapters 1 to 6 and the Conclusion.

Biographers tend to assume
that what makes people who they are now
made people who they were then.
Historians are not so sure.

—JAMES SHAPIRO,
1599: A Year in the Life of William Shakespeare

An artist is really just the precondition of his work,
the womb, the soil, and sometimes the dung and manure,
in which and out of which his work grows—
and so usually a thing you have to forget,
if you want to enjoy the work itself . . .
Homer wouldn't have created Achilles, or Goethe Faust,
if Homer had *been* Achilles, or Goethe Faust.

—FRIEDRICH NIETZSCHE,
On the Genealogy of Morals: iii, 4

INTRODUCTION

THE FACE, THE FACTS AND THE PORN, OR WHY WE MUST STOP CONDESCENDING TO THE PAST

The Icon of the Myth.

The Face of Kafka

You know the face I mean, of course. Everyone does. There are many photos of Dr. Franz Kafka (1883–1924) but, as far as Prague souvenirs and English-language biographies go, this might as well be the only one.

Now, this is very unusual for a writer. Who would bet on being able to finger Flaubert, Stendhal, Dostoyevsky, James, Conrad, and Proust in an identification parade of random upper-middle-class men of the past? And why should anyone care to? They are remembered for their books, not their looks. Dickens has a memorable hairstyle, true, and a couple of other modern author photos have become local tourist icons for the cities they fled (Dublin makes a fine old effort with James Joyce, and Swansea tries with Dylan Thomas), but Kafka is in a different international league. Apart from Shakespeare, there's simply *no* writer whose image is so well known to so many people who have never read a word he wrote. The face of Kafka has become virtually a brand.

Not that Kafka doesn't deserve his fame. If ever mankind gets to the stars, people commuting between planets will know of his work. I spent ten years of my life studying that work, teaching it at universities, publishing articles on it in weighty journals—and I can't think of many better ways to spend ten years.*

But Kafka's fame is strange. Dante, Shakespeare, Goethe, Keats, Flaubert, Dickens, Chekhov, Proust, Joyce are all *quoted.* It's their *words* that count, which, since words were all they left behind them, seems pretty logical. Kafka's words are probably quoted less often than those of any other writer of his rank: he is world famous for his *visions.*

You can see why: A man wakes up and finds that he's a beetle. A man who has done nothing wrong fights for his life against a bizarre court that sits in almost every attic in the world. A machine quite literally writes condemned people to death. A man tries forever to get into a mysterious castle. A man waits in vain all his life by the Door to the Law, only to be told as he dies that this door was only ever meant for him. These visions haunt the world like those of no other self-conscious, modern author. They have the cthonic power of mysterious fragments from a lost scroll of the Pentateuch or a tantalizingly half-preserved Greek myth.

Yet no image becomes immortal just because it's a great High Concept. The dustbin of literary history is filled with the wrecks of ideas that looked great on the backs of envelopes. Every half-cultured Westerner has at least vaguely heard of Don Quixote and his windmills, but no one would know of this vision today if Cer-

*See (if you insist), J. M. Hawes, *Nietzsche and the End of Freedom, the neo-Romantic Dilemma in Kafka, the Brothers Mann, Rilke and Musil*, Frankfurt (Lang) 1993; 'Blind Resistance? A reply to Elizabeth Boa's reading of Kafka's *Auf der Galerie*' in *Deutsche Vierteljahrsschrift für Literaturwissenschaft und Geistesgeschichte*, 69. Jahrgang, Heft 2/June 1995, pp.324–36; The Psychology of Power in Kafka's *Der Process* and Heinrich Mann's *Der Untertan*, in *Oxford German Studies* 17/18 (1990), pp.119–31; *Faust* and Nietzsche in Kafka's *Der Process*, in *New German Studies* 15/2, 1989.

vantes had just sent it out as a witty one-liner. It lives only because it's part of a larger whole that *worked for the people who first
read it*—and was therefore transmitted down to the next generation, who agreed, and so on.

What counts, in other words, is not only the tale but also the
telling. This is where the K.-myth comes in—or, rather, gets in
the way. It continually pushes the idea of a mysterious genius, a
lonely Middle European Nostradamus, who, almost ignored by
his contemporaries, somehow plumbed the depths of his mysterious, quasi-saintly psyche to predict the Holocaust and the Gu-
lags. The brooding face of Kafka has become the icon of that
K.-myth and his name, typographically irresistible to anyone
from west of the Rhine *(my dear, that mysterious Z, that oh-so-non-
Western double K!)* has entered the languages of the world in the
term kafkaesque, used wherever guiltless people are trapped in
some nightmarish bureaucratic catch-22.

In the very simplest of ways, we can see that it's only a myth.
That photo, overwhelmingly the most famous image of him, the
international trademark of Prague (which Kafka longed for years
to escape), was actually taken in a department store in Berlin
(which he longed for years to get to). It's also the last picture of
him ever taken. This is loading the dice somewhat. What we now
know as the face of Kafka was created about eight months before
his death, when he knew logically that he was doomed (he compared his move to Berlin to Napoleon's invasion of Russia) but
had not quite given up on the irrational hope of still finding real,
human life and love.

This state of mind is (a) typical of his writing and (b) liable to
make anyone look profound.

But still not profound enough. The legendary Kafka collector
and publisher Klaus Wagenbach recalls watching in the early
fifties as the S. Fischer Co. artists retouched this picture to give
Kafka's eyes the desired gleam. And it worked. *Prophetic Kafka* is

now as famous and vague an icon as *Saintly Che Guevara*—and with about as much historical accuracy.

Faces are not just faces; they carry stories. Evolution has minutely tuned our attention to what they say. The whole modern visually driven circus of media stardom depends on our ancient hominid instincts to note and judge incredibly precise facial details. So even if you've never read a word of Kafka, you'll feel— you won't be able to help feeling—that, since you know his icon, you know something about him.

As far as I can tell, most English-speakers seem to pick up Kafka's writings vaguely expecting something like a mixture of Edgar Allan Poe, *The Fly*, Philip K. Dick, and *1984*. No other writer's work suffers from this kind of prejudgment. It means that readers come to Kafka already beholding the (alleged) man, forgetting that in the beginning were his words.

But there are biographies, guidebooks, and essay-writing aids aplenty, never mind the practically infinite mass of academic interpretation that has gathered around this physically modest corpus of work (never in the history of literary scholarship have so many written so much about so little). So surely, it's easy to get to know more about Kafka before taking the supposedly heavy plunge into his actual works. Probably, you already know some of these "facts" yourself:

- Kafka's will ordered that all his works should be destroyed.
- Kafka was virtually unknown in his lifetime, partly because he was shy about publishing.
- Kafka was terrified of his brutal father.
- Kafka was crushed by a dead-end bureaucratic job.
- Kafka was crippled for years by the TB that he knew must inevitably kill him.
- Kafka was incredibly honest about his failings with the women in his life—*too* honest.

- Kafka was imprisoned, as a German-speaking Jew in Prague, in a double ghetto: a minority-within-a-minority amid an absurd and collapsing operetta-like empire.
- Kafka's works are based on his experiences as a Jew.
- Kafka's works uncannily predict Auschwitz.
- Kafka's works were burned by the Nazis.

These are the building blocks of the K.-myth. Unfortunately, they are all rubbish—so much so that, at present, it's drastic but true to say that the *less* you know about Kafka's alleged life the *greater* chance you have of enjoying his superb writing.

This is just as true for most people who are formally taught about Kafka at school or college. What is taught at most institutions is just a version of the above rubbish. Two generations of adoring biographers and theorizing academics have churned out an image of perfect human profundity (which moves books) and unfathomable literary/psychological complexity (which sells research proposals). Do they care to represent the real Dr. Franz Kafka (1883–1924)? No, thank you. Really, they are in the same game as the sellers of tourist knickknacks in Prague. All they want is K., a face-and-name icon that will bring, through the doors of their shops or lecture halls, people who have never read his writings, a brand to hang their businesses and theories on.

In the last few years, the very best Kafka people have at last begun to argue against this comfortable rubbish. This book is indebted deeply to them.* However, it's a tough job.

Scholarly discussions can all too easily (and often, quite rightly) be dismissed as mere insider pitches for grants, jobs, and research posts. If there's one idea that resounds through Kafka's writing, it's that rational arguments, however objectively true

---

*See *Further Reading*. The most important (as will be seen from the number of times I refer to it) is Peter-André Alt's *Der ewige Sohn*. It's crazy that this mighty biography, which makes all others obsolete, is still unavailable in English.

they may be, simply bounce right off the stories we *want* to believe.

In his own case, the K.-myth is so spectacularly fake you have to conclude that a lot of people really, really *want* that myth rather than the facts. And when you're going after people's beloved idols, the only way to philosophize is with a hammer or, to use Kafka's image rather than Nietzsche's, with an axe to break the frozen sea of Kafka studies.

So this book isn't going to *argue* that the K.-myth has wildly skewed our view of Kafka and his writings. It's going to *show* it—where necessary, by using some long-lost dynamite that no one, not even the best modern German scholars, has ever used before.

We'll see how the K.-myth has so blinded scholars that, despite all the hundreds or thousands of PhDs awarded on Kafka, not *one* of them, not even the latest Germans, has ever noticed that Kafka's most famous single image—*that* beetle—is the cultural equivalent of James Joyce's quoting the opening scene of *Hamlet* at the start of *Ulysses*.*

We'll see Kafka himself, saying that he "simply imitated" Dickens and took his observational method from Sherlock Holmes. We'll see him reducing his first listeners (as well as himself) to *helpless laughter* as he reads the most famous opening of any twentieth-century novel. We'll see him being pushed by a powerful literary clique. We'll see him, a high-ranking Jew in the service of a militaristic, authoritarian German-speaking empire that ruled a Czech-speaking country, quite literally investing in victory over the Allies.

And we'll see what two entire generations of scholars have *never shown* to Kafka's readers, the stuff that Kafka himself (quite understandably) kept hidden away in his locked bookcase and which his acolytes have made sure has stayed safely locked away ever

---

*I couldn't believe this myself at first. So I checked with Professor Ritchie Robertson, Chair of German at Oxford University, Britain's undisputed Kafka Champion.

since. Pictures that, when I first saw them, made me rub my eyes, then quickly take the files for this book off the family PC desktop and save them where my two preteen boys wouldn't come across them. Kafka's porn.

The past won't be condescended to. In 1907, a public glimpse of stocking was shocking, since respectable women such as Ms. Felice Bauer still dressed according to a code that would essentially pass muster with today's Islamic vigilantes. So when Kafka's contemporaries, Joyce and Conrad, give us comic scenes of sneaky porn-buying in *Ulysses* and *The Secret Agent*, modern readers are apt to assume that these are cases of laughably harmless "naughty" stuff. But the images that Kafka himself ordered, paid for, and kept carefully hidden away would, even today, put the journals firmly on the top shelf. It may well be illegal for you to look at them if you're under eighteen (or, indeed at all, in certain lands).

But that's the whole point. Only if we stop condescending to the past will we ever see Kafka as he really was, allowing us to sidestep the K.-myth and read his works afresh, not just as mighty one-liners but as the splendid and often surprising works they really are. Works that did not spring from timeless subterranean depths but have a quite clear ancestry and place within the story of Western literature.

So let's start with a look at one day in the life this man and his world—a world that was once just as real as ours, but which is now utterly, almost unimaginably lost. A look at the way things once really *were* . . .

THE WAY THINGS WERE

Wer will, daß wir siegen,
zeichnet
Kriegsanleihe.

"Whoever wants us to be victorious will buy war bonds."

In Which an Ancient State Offers a Canny Investment, Attracting (Among Others) a Certain Bohemian-German Lawyer and Businessman

It is the afternoon of Friday, November 5, 1915, and we are in the center of Prague, the many-spired, history-ridden capital of the Kingdom of Bohemia, third-largest city in the Austro-Hungarian Empire.

Lying smack on the main railway line (indeed, virtually midway) between Berlin and Vienna, Prague (a popular tourist destination in peacetime) is not only the capital of Kaiser Franz Josef's most important industrial region but a vital geographic link in the alliance between Europe's two German-speaking powers.

The war dominates the news, of course. Today's issue of the *Prague Daily News,* the city's widely respected newspaper, carries reports and maps of (still more) victories, as well as a long and gloating transcript of the acrimonious parliamentary debates in

London about the Gallipoli debacle.* But life goes on, and the paper also has the usual stock exchange reports (wheat and railways were lively on neutral Wall Street yesterday, but steel shares took hits and cotton is slow), the everyday advertisements (cabarets and cinemas in Prague, hotels in Berlin) and cultural snippets (the latest Parisian innovation is the "cinematic novel," in which a story is to be shown in daily episodes). And as for the future, well, sprinkled throughout the paper are banners and articles urging people to invest in the third issue of Austrian war bonds, which offer a guaranteed 5.5 percent, tax free for fifteen years—but whose lists close for good at midday tomorrow, Saturday. Thick columns are filled with the names of those who've already signed up.

And no wonder: 5.5 percent! That's almost a whole percent and a half more than French and German government bonds were yielding before the war, an income guaranteed for fifteen years and *completely tax free*. Who can resist? Even a group of Prague schoolchildren, reports the *Daily News*, have collected together one hundred crowns to buy a bond, the interest of which will be used in future to help poor pupils from their district. Rich or poor, people should think hard, says the paper: after all, what kind of risky investments would you normally have to make, to hope for *that* kind of return? Whereas now you have the chance to get something copper bottomed, cast iron, gilt edged, and better, for these bonds are not issued by some fly-by-night limited company, but by the state itself.

And the state that has issued them is no mere two-bit republic but the Habsburg Empire, fief of Europe's grandest dynasty, the family who defeated the Turks at Lepanto and saved the Christian world, whose armadas sailed to reconvert England, who the Catholic

---

*As ever, an authoritarian and censored society sees its enemies' public fallings-out as sure evidence of impending collapse.

A canny investment, 1915.

Church sees as its greatest bastion and of whose royal line the latest king-emperor, Franz Josef, has reigned here for so long that it feels like forever.

Millions of Franz Josef's multinational subjects have been born, led their lives, and passed on without ever knowing any other ruler. The silver-haired old men holding up their grandsons, perhaps even their great-grandsons, to see the famous regiments of the Royal and Imperial Army as they march off to end this war in victory, are *huzzah*-ing the very same, by now almost unearthly sovereign they knew themselves as children. It is almost impossible even to imagine a world without Franz Josef, never mind without the Habsburg Empire.

A safe investment? What could be safer? Companies fall, even banks can break, but empires? Yes, of course, war is always a risky business, and it may not have been the Habsburg forte since Prince Eugene saved Europe from the Turks (again)—but then, it never really was their way, for as the ancient Latin motto says: *Bella gerant alli, tu felix Austria nube* (Other lands by war are made/You, happy Austria, get engaged). Even when Austria has taken to the field and been beaten, by a Frederick the Great, a Napoleon or a Bismarck, there has always been a Habsburg sitting there proudly at the table, once the gunsmoke fades, the armies disband, and the powers assemble once again, their rulers generally cousins of some kind, in some glittering palace or other, to haggle over the peace and tinker with the map of Europe.* Someone loses a province, someone gains one, but the great nations remain. And in any case, Austria (who started this whole war) isn't going to lose any provinces, not this time, not to Serbia or Russia or anyone else, because her latest marriage (even if it was something of a shotgun wedding following the bloody humiliation of 1866) to her newly rich neighbor, the hyperdynamic German Empire, has proved once again that our canny old king-emperor knows the real first law of warfare: choose the right allies.

In the opening months of the war, true, things had looked less certain. The euphoria that had swept the Habsburg domains as powerfully as it had every country in Europe (even Dr. Sigmund

---

*And the notorious Habsburg Secret Police (the model for the czars' version, thus eventually for Lenin's and Stalin's version) will be taking notes on everyone. They even spied on Goethe when he happened to be in Vienna during the Congress of 1815.

Freud stopped analyzing and gave himself up to feeling "truly Austrian" for once) soon evaporated. The problem was—when *wasn't* it?—the Russians.

The Russians had kept Germany and Austria safe for monarchy in 1848–49, when the newly crowned Franz Josef had accepted their help. Wily old Count Bismarck always bent over backward to keep them onside (as Frederick the Great had advised, even he having been shocked by the barbarity of war against them). But Bismarck's complex system of treaties was allowed to lapse by the young Kaiser Wilhelm and his advisers. Nowadays, in this new world driven by nationalist passions, France may still be the inherited enemy and the German Navy may toast what they simply call the Day, the coming reckoning with England, but it's the Russians, with their limitless manpower and their vague but persistent claims to speak for all Slavs everywhere (many millions of whom live under German or Austrian masters) who *really* scare Berlin and Vienna.

Hence the Germans' famous Schlieffen Plan, which treated victory in the West as a mere preliminary. That France would be beaten was certain: what mattered was knocking France out before the gigantic but inefficient Romanov war machine could trundle into action, so that the whole strength of German arms could steam quickly back across the Reich, to be turned on the real and deadly foe.

Russia, however, threw caution, codebooks, and, as it turned out, her own future to the wind, mobilizing and attacking more swiftly than the German General Staff, those legendary station-masters of modern warfare, had calculated to be humanly possible. Czar Nicholas's armies marched into both German and Austro-Hungarian lands. Refugees flooded into Berlin, Vienna, and Prague, their fearful cry, the wail of all Central European liberals back in 1848, spreading panic: "The Cossacks are coming!" Kaiser

Wilhelm's spike-helmeted paladins wavered. Their precious strategy survived first contact with the enemy no better than any military plan ever has. Directly contradicting Schlieffen's legendary dying words—"Just keep the right wing strong!"—they hurriedly redeployed vital divisions eastward.*

However, the crisis passed: Hindenburg and Ludendorff knocked the wheels off the dreaded Russian steamroller at Tannenberg, making themselves into national heroes; the long-despised Turks have given the perfidious British a bloody nose in the Dardanelles; and despite the insane cascade of lives thrown at it by the French, the unbeatable German Army, its trenches deep in enemy soil, is so confidently absorbing the pressure that it can now transfer forces eastward at will, to the fraternal aid of Austria.

And what aid mighty Germany gives her friends! Six months ago, in May 1915, a joint German/Austrian army group under General (now promoted to Field Marshall) von Mackensen of the Death's Head Hussars utterly smashed the Russian front in the greatest battle of the war, the rout of Gorlice-Tarnow. The victory unfolded under the All-Highest gaze, for Kaiser Wilhelm, reported the Berlin press, sped by automobile to visit his cheering soldiers on the very battlefield.

The spectacular campaign of summer 1915, unleashed by this triumph of Teutonic unity, has been very different from the meat-grinding horror of the Western Front. Czar Nicholas's hordes have been flung back hundreds of miles, shattered and reeling, clean out of his Polish domains and even beyond, into Russia proper. On August 5, Warsaw fell, followed by the fortress town of Kovno and proud Ivangorod. On September 5, Nicholas sacked his cousin Grand Duke Nikolai and took personal command of his armies, to confront "the invasion of the enemy." But on September 18, Vil-

---

*See Barbara Tuchmann's *August 1914*, which is not only the best book ever written on the opening of the Great War but one of the best books ever written about anything.

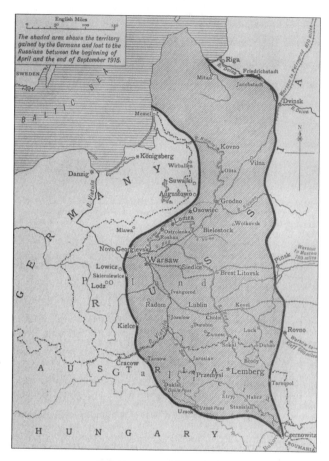

Mitteleuropa transformed, 1915.

nius fell, too. Since May, Russia has lost several entire armies and prosperous, well-developed territories roughly the size of England.

The world is watching these great events closely, and drawing its own conclusions. King 'Foxy' Ferdinand of Bulgaria was courted by France, Britain, and Russia with increasing ardor this summer as the Eastern Front collapsed and the casualties mounted at Gallipoli (a desperate secret memorandum for the British PM pleaded that only "the certain co-operation of Bulgaria" could justify the continued slaughter there).

But when Bulgaria at last joined in, it was not on the side of her supposed Slav brothers and their allies. Just three weeks ago, on October 11, Ferdinand's prime minister left the world in no doubt why Bulgaria has finally jumped the way she has:

> One recognizes more clearly day by day that victory is inclining on the side of Germany and Austria-Hungary . . . it has become clear to the point of certainty for every observer that Russia will soon be overthrown, and then the turn will come for France, England, Italy and Serbia.

Indeed, Belgrade has since already gone the way of Warsaw. In fact, the political map of Europe has been transformed this summer. All Middle Europe is at last firmly in Germanic hands!

True, Italy has been bribed to join in on the side of France and Britain, but what does the feeble hostility of Italy (whose attacks have so far made no progress at high cost) weigh compared to the thrashing of the Imperial Russian Army? Now, the refugees from the borderlands with Russia are returning home (a trainload of Galician Jews set off back from Prague only yesterday) and Russian prisoners are being officially offered as language teachers to businessmen, for, as the *Prague Daily News* points out today, trade between Bohemia and Russia will soon blossom again, simply because the Russians will obviously be in no position to fulfill their own industrial needs after this war!

Yes, the heady days of August 1914 may be gone, and victory may be taking longer than expected, but on cool reflection it's nonetheless pretty clear to any thinking person that the world-historical die has been cast. Russia has been kicked right out of Europe proper—along with the pan-Slav, Jew-baiting fantasies that have disturbed Prague in recent decades. Decadent France, the land of the anti-Semitic Dreyfus scandal, is going to finally have to see that a nation of forty million cannot be Europe's natural leader when a nation of sixty-three million (seventy-five million if you count Austria's Germans) wants its place in the sun. England's arrogant global empire has been revealed as sclerotic and impotent, vaunted Royal Navy and all: no ship, not even the mighty *Lusitania*, is safe from Germany's U-boats and London herself is now under attack from the stupendous zeppelins.

America may be manifestly destined to rule across the Atlantic, but in the Old World it is Germanic spirit and technology that are clearly triumphant, as if evolution itself were at work in this storm of steel.

Certainly, it may well be that this is going to mean Austria taking a distinctly subordinate role to Germany—but, after all, German is as German speaks, really, and where Krupp's unstoppable guns blast a path, there will surely follow in their train that matchless artistic/scientific *Kultur* in which Austria can claim her full and glorious part (and of which the loyal Jewish subjects of Hohenzollern and Habsburg can be especially proud): that extraordinary Greater German culture that defined the nineteenth century and is already revolutionizing the twentieth, that incomparable roll call of Haydn, Mozart, and Beethoven; of Goethe, Schiller, and Kleist; of Hoffman, Grillparzer, and Heine; of Schubert, Schumann, and Mendelssohn; of Wagner, Liszt, and Brahms; of Schopenhauer, Nietzsche, and Marx; of Sigmund Freud, Max Planck, and Albert Einstein . . .

The inscrutable but irresistible forces that Hegel divined as the motors of world history have made their decision: from the Rhine to the Bug, from the Alps to the Fjords, from the Baltic and the North Sea to the Adriatic and the Black Sea, and who knows how far beyond, this is going to be the *German* century.

In short, the Habsburgs, Europe's great survivors, have wedded wisely yet again. And so how can any prudent investor now resist their latest guaranteed war bonds? Little wonder the last issue of Berlin's equivalent (which closed in September) was so overwhelmingly successful that Kaiser Wilhelm was moved to publish a personal message of thanks to his people, comparing the event to a major victory of arms. I mean, think about it again: 5.5 percent, guaranteed for fifteen years and *tax free*! Who's going to be offering *that*, on a cast-iron investment, once the war is won and the defeated entente being forced to pay for it all (as the French were made to foot the bill after 1871)? Patriotism and profit, hand in hand—but only until lunchtime tomorrow.

Tempted? You should be.*

It's certainly enough to attract a certain thirty-two-year-old Prague lawyer and businessman, himself named by his ex-sergeant-major father in loyal honor of the emperor, who is, right now, on this afternoon of November 5, 1915, dithering outside the war bonds outlet.

In Which We Meet Our Hero, a Highly Respected Insurance Expert Too Important for the Trenches

As our hero decides what to do about the war bonds, no doubt many passersby greet him with a polite: *"Guten Tag, Herr Doktor!"* for one way or another he knows pretty well everyone who is anyone in the small circle of the German-Bohemians (as they call themselves) of Prague. They were still a majority here just about within living memory, but now they make up less than 10 percent of the population, so they stick together.

Perhaps, as one of them, you tip your hat overrespectfully in error, thinking it's his cousin Bruno, of the same name, almost his spitting image, an even more successful doctor of law in Prague, editor of the *Prague Daily News*'s even more hyperpatriotic rival, *Bohemia,* and one of the recognized leaders of your German-

*The Grand Prior of the Knights of St. John of Malta was. He liquidated vast amounts of his legendary Order's ancient holdings and put the lot into these very war bonds.

speaking community. But our hero is well known in his own right, too, as the son of a noted local businessman, from his wide-ranging official legal work and through his involvement with the family's asbestos factory.

If you belong to the upper reaches of the Germans here, you may well have met him socially, as a fellow member of wealthy Bertha Fanta's exclusive salon, where the latest intellectual and artistic developments are presented in an intimate social milieu by such luminaries as Dr. Rudolf Steiner* and Dr. Albert Einstein[†]. You may have bumped into him in one of the city's upscale cafés or nightclubs (or, indeed, brothels).

If you're Jewish—and as a German-speaking *Volksgenosse* (folk comrade) in Prague, the odds are that you *are* Jewish—you might have heard of his slightly bizarre championing of the despised Yiddish theater (as opposed to the respectable German theater), but it's very unlikely you've seen him at synagogue because he virtually never goes. He can't see much point in going along with the empty formalities of assimilated religion—especially when everyone knows damn well that the man over there in the congregation is the owner of a brothel.[1] As for the Eastern Jews who fled here in 1914, there's no doubt that they actually mean it, but their rites seem to him like those of a "wild African tribe" and a pair of young refugee girls whom he desires right now (their parents won't let things get anywhere) make him think of "deepest Asia."[2]

At any rate, synagogue-goer or not, it's quite likely that you, as a fellow German-speaking *Prager*, know who he is, and that he's a man worth tipping one's hat to.

He stands out in any crowd, never mind a wartime one where

---

*Founder of the schools beloved by the would-be-artistic middle classes to this day. Our hero's gentle, deadly mockery of Steiner (and of himself for ever having thought Steiner worth talking to) is a comic highlight of the early diaries (28 March 1911).

[†]Whose wife later claimed that her husband and our hero became close enough in Prague for him to have visited their home in Berlin years later. But until someone proves it, this wonderful scenario must remain an early piece of celeb-wife gossip.

Our hero, 1915.

young, fit men out of uniform are becoming a rarity. At just under six feet tall, he's a whole head taller than the average man in the street, with big dark eyes and a skin almost olive in complexion, handsome, spruce, and fit looking. As well he might be, for he swims, rows, and bicycles. He doesn't smoke; is teetotal; won't touch coffee, tea, or even chocolate. He insists on only the freshest of vegetarian food and is even fussy about the *way* he eats it, for he religiously *Fletcherizes*—a fashionable though somewhat antisocial dietary method (also used by J. P. Rockefeller) named after the man who invented the worldwide fad, San Francisco art dealer Horace Fletcher, the "great masticator." It involves chewing each mouthful for so long that it is reduced to a sort of self-swallowing soup, thus extracting (sayeth Fletcher) the maximum nutrition at minimal strain to the digestion! He worries at the thought of his ex-fiancée not remotely Fletcherizing her unhealthy Berlin city diet.

As well as Fletcherizing every meal, he *Müllerizes* for ten minutes every day. That is, he dutifully carries out, as he has done for years, a program of the latest scientific calisthenic exercises, performed in as little clothing as possible before an open window, according to the instructions set out in his well-thumbed copy of *Mein System*—the international bestseller by "the most beautiful man of the new century," Jens Peter Müller, the famous Nordic (and nudist) bodybuilder, from whom copies of Müller's signature Greek-style bodybuilding sandals may be purchased by mail order.

No wonder the Herr Doktor passed the Royal and Imperial Austrian Army's medical board just this June, for the second time.

He had confided to his secret diary on May 14 that he feared a heart condition might make him fail, and had written to his ex-fiancée on the twenty-seventh that he "yet" hoped to be called up. As it happens, he was declared "fully useable" and fit for infantry service. But he hasn't been called up, because as a highflier in a major semistate institution, he is regarded as so irreplaceable that his bosses have once more insisted he be kept out of the war.

Like most people in Reserved Occupations, he feels occasional pangs of unsoldierly shame: tomorrow he's going to visit the mother of his one-time best friend, the only man he ever really tried to make like him, who was killed in June. He's also occasionally prone to buy into the romantic idea of the "front-line experience," the brotherhood of comradeship as a panacea for psychological ills, as hymned in *The Great Year 1914–1915* from the Berlin publisher Fischer, in which the firm's cultural big shots, such as Thomas Mann (whose books our hero greatly likes), line up to extol the idea.[3] But although he's more than once said he wants to go, he hasn't gone so far as to report as a free-will volunteer. Now, he feels that, by signing up for the buying of bonds, he is really taking part in the war.

He weighs the prospects for the war bonds as far as he can judge them. He can certainly do so better than most people, for he is by no means an innocent when it comes to assessing financial risks; that is, after all, a central part of his job. He helped drive through a major restructuring of his deficit-ridden institute a few years ago, and was instrumental in persuading his extended family to set up their asbestos business.[4]

Moreover, as a classically educated university man, he is well able to take in the long view of things, the big picture, too: just five weeks ago, perhaps inspired by the endless press reports of stunning German-Austrian gains on the Eastern Front, he was making page upon page of orderly notes in his private diary about how Bonaparte's Grande Armée (and thus Napoleon himself, who

Kafka on the Beach, July 1914.

has long rather fascinated him) could have won, or at least survived, the fatal Russian campaign of 1812.

He has never doubted that even if Austria, herself, should tremble, Germany would pull both nations through. Last July, he passed right through Germany on the way home from a beach holiday in Denmark and was impressed by the calm firmness of its population in the face of possible war.

And this April, on a trip to Hungary, he was frankly awed by the sight of a gigantic German officer marching across the platform and through the train, so stiff with discipline and greatness that it seemed incredible he could still actually move at all.

The events of summer have fully borne out his profound trust in German power. Like the wily Bulgarians, he can only see one side winning this war—which makes these bonds a safe bet to deliver a very useful income right up to the day in November 1930 when they'll be paid back in full by a grateful State.

The fact is that he has, for years now, been working out how he could ever afford to give up his day job. Might this be the key? The asbestos factory, for all the money and time he and his family have put into it, largely at his own instigation, is now certainly not going to deliver (and may even leave all concerned with big debts, as his father often reminds him).

If only (as his best friend put it in a letter to our hero's then-fiancée) his tight-fisted parents would treat him like a daughter and gave him a sort of "dowry" to let him take a few gap-years in the Mediterranean! Or if he could be more like his poet friend Franz Werfel, the star of the Café Arco, whom he envies to the point of hatred (as he admitted to his diary four years ago) because "he is healthy, young and rich—all of which I am not."

Will nothing ever free him from the office?*

In Which Our Hero Considers His Career, Marriage, and Bachelorhood

Choosing to study law and to then get fixed up with a pensionable career in the fast-track senior ranks of the civil service had just seemed the natural, sensible thing to do. His parents are comfortably off, they let him study whatever he wanted at college, but they worked hard for it all, they still do, and Dad never tires of telling him just *how* hard). His mother wrote in secret to his girlfriend (later his fiancée) on November 16, 1912, saying that anyone else would be "the happiest man alive" to have such a job.

---

*In 1911 the average worker in one of the factories our hero inspected as part of his work earned around 1000 crowns per year. Full board at the high-end Jungborn nudist resort-cum-sanatorium cost just under 10 crowns per day. Taken all in all, I'd suggest we must imagine 1 crown = *at least* $15 to give some rough idea of a modern U.S. equivalent. On this basis, our hero's salary of 5,796 crowns in November 1915 must be thought of as least $90,000 (regularly rising and utterly secure) for his six hours per day—and the apartment-block which his father bought outright in January 1918 (for 500,000 Crowns) as worth at least $7,500,000. How wealthy you *feel* may indeed depend on how rich your friends are, but by any objective standard our hero and his family are very comfortably off.

Because really, if one has to earn a living, his job at the Arbeiter-Unfall-Versicherungs-Anstalt für das Königreich Böhmen (the Workers' Accident Insurance Institute for the Kingdom of Bohemia) is about as good as a salaried job gets. It has the social cachet and the absolute security of a fairly senior (and rising) position in the service of the all-powerful state. It also has that highly enviable state-sector schedule (a mere six-hour day, whereas in the private sector he worked eight or nine). Leaving the office at two P.M. is a massive plus. He works hard and has made his mark, helped by the fact that, unusually for a German-speaker, he also has pretty fluent Czech (which counts, what with the new political correctness, imposed from Vienna, about Czech being an equal language). He's been regularly and speedily promoted, he publicly represents the institute in courts and conferences—all in all, there's no doubt that he's a favorite of his bosses. And they are good bosses to have, too: not stressed-out modern business types permanently shouting into phones or dictating machines (or at their inferiors) as his superiors did in the private sector, but civilized, educated men in the grand old European tradition of high state mandarins.

They are also, of course, not unaware that our hero has a good deal of *Protektion* here. Having been good school friends with the son of the house, he's on visiting terms with their boss of bosses, Herr President Dr. Pribram, himself. Naturally, there are no rules that say anything about giving that little bit more time and consideration to a clever, hard-working, likeable friend of the Herr President's son. Even more naturally, there don't have to be. The rules that *really* matter are always unwritten, aren't they?

Well, for whatever reason, Herr Direktor Marschner is quite capable of listening to our hero's strange dreams or sitting down with him to recite the great German-Jewish poet Heine at each other, head to head, during business hours, even while there are messengers, departmental heads, and clients waiting right outside

Our hero on a mock-up plane ride (with two of his reviewers and the sister
of a future publisher), Vienna 1913.

the door.[5] When his two bosses needed to address a vast insurance
industry conference in Vienna two years ago, he practically wrote
both their speeches (and was invited along for the jaunt as a re-
ward).

In peacetime, they had allowed him extra vacation days when
he'd complained of nervous stress, and now they not only keep
him out of the trenches but have even approved a whopping raise
for him this year, war or no war.

In fact, many people would kill for a job like his. That makes
it pretty hard to explain why he wants to give it up so badly.

She didn't understand, for example. She who is still always on
his mind. His ex-fiancée. They almost married last year. She's
twenty-seven years old now, a modern, big-city Berlin girl, an executive in a cutting-edge firm making and selling the latest high-
tech dictation systems.

Our hero's ex-fiancée and her product.

Perhaps they can make things work after all? She obviously really loves him. She must, if she's even remotely *thinking* about trying again after the horrendous breakup in Berlin last summer (oh God, that meeting with her parents, where it all came out as if he were standing in court, all that business about him and her best friend. Talk about grounds for a lawsuit!).

Does he want marriage, a home, a family? Of course. On the day four years ago when the family's lawyer (another distant relative of the same name) was setting up the paperwork for the new asbestos factory, a clause came up that dealt with his possible future wife and children: he suddenly noticed a nearby table with one large and two small chairs set at it, all empty, and the thought that he'd never be able to fill those chairs with that wife and kids filled him with desperate longing. As his beloved Flaubert said, a man looking after a family is living real life, life *"dans le vrai."*

In theory, anyway. But what if *real life* actually means *a life like Mom and Dad's?* Anything but that! Last summer, 1914, he'd gotten as far as apartment hunting and choosing furniture with his fiancée. She'd chosen solid, heavy, respectable Berlin things that had made him imagine he could hear a death knell sounding in

Our hero's favorite furniture.

the furniture factory, whereas he'd wanted the latest lightweight designer stuff made in a garden suburb of Dresden.

God, that furniture business still rankles!* Perhaps he's just not meant for a respectable, normal life. The fact is, before he met her (and even for a while afterward) he enjoyed an active nightlife of the sort that delivered "opportunities" so naturally and easily that one could almost kid oneself it was all happening by accident. Opportunities to meet younger, less sophisticated, and, well, you know, more *instinctive* girls. Shop girls, factory girls, typists, maids: there are plenty of poor, rootless young things in Prague . . .

And if you can't be bothered even with easy Viennese-style schmoozing in some cabaret or bar, well, there are many upscale brothels in Prague, as he knows very well (he's also visited establishments in Paris and Milan, and Leipzig). Everyone does it.

Although maybe not everyone has felt themselves passing a bordello "like a lover passing his sweetheart's house" or more recently, going "deliberately down the alleys where the tarts are, en-

---

*Why was it so important? We shall see later.

A Prague waitress in her day-off finery,
early twentieth century.

joying the distant but nonetheless real possibility of going with one"—and wanting "only the old, fat ones."[6]

And not everyone used to read and hide away such journals as *The Amethyst* and *Opals*.*

But that's the whole point. Brothels and streetwalkers, porn and easy sweethearts, or wandering the streets and just *looking* dreamily at girls, at their clothes, hair, legs, ears, and accessories, as he often does, are all very well when you're a young professional in your twenties, carefree, single, and living at home like everyone else.†

---

*See Part II: *Into the Locked Bookcase.*

†No respectable person leaves the family home to live *alone* without pressing logic of career or trade. Why on earth *would* they? (This is still common-sense to most of the Earth's population: it is we "Westerners", like K. in *The Castle*, obsessed with individual fulfillment at all cost, who are, as humans, statistically the weirdos).

Now he's thirty-two. Who wants to end up the last unhitched man in town?

Has he missed the boat? All his friends are married now, and a married friend's not a real friend anymore, not for a single man. He knows a few older men who've ended up alone and he can all too easily conjure up their lonely lives, their quiet apartments, their secret desperation. Even his uncle Alfred, a very successful man, indeed (and one whose backing has helped his own career), almost openly admits to this. Imagine: Admiring other people's children and having to remind yourself that you have none. Having to practically beg when you just want to spend an evening with other humans. Your life growing narrower and narrower until, in the end, a coffin is just the right fit. One day he could find himself not just imagining all this, but actually *living* it, hitting his hand on his forehead and wondering how it came to this. What's the point living like that? How can you justify a mad, empty bachelor life?

He's still in regular touch with Felice. This March, he'd pointed out that with his fat new salary hike under his belt (the raise alone is about an ordinary working man's wages), the outlook could be pretty rosy for them after the war. He'd looked wistfully out of his own lonely window across at the morning sunlight shining on the three windows of the very apartment they'd wanted to rent. What would *she* have said to those windows, he'd sorrowfully asked her? This Whitsun (Pentecost) they'd met for the first time since the breakup; again in Karlsbad in June. For weeks afterward, he (who has so often complained about the noise and bustle at his parents') found himself dreading being alone in his room.

No, no, no, best not to even *think* about the land of elderly bachelors going up their lonely staircases to their lonely flats. Who wants to know what they have battering about in their secret cupboards? Let's just say: when he says a "mad bachelor life," *mad* is *exactly* what he means. Two months ago, he could see only two cures: Felice—or the Front.

Perhaps, if she's still interested now, they could, after all, find some way of building a kind of normal life, like she wants, like *he* needs, too—but one that'll still give him the peace and time he needs to really *do* something with his life. But how? Not as long as she can't resist telling him to "make something" of the asbestos factory (as she did yet again this January), that's for sure!

He needs to get things sorted out because if he's ever going to really chase his dreams, he needs to do it right now. You get one chance, then the door shuts in your face and, if you missed it, tough. Yes, going through that door is a scary prospect, one that would mean him going full tilt for a life his family would all call crazy, and perhaps quite rightly. But then, what would a *not-crazy* life mean? To give up, sit down by the side of the big door, and just rot away . . . ?

This image of waiting hopelessly by a door (which Nietzsche, whom he greatly admired in his youth, also employed) haunts him, and he used it in a little story (actually, the heart of something much bigger that he just wasn't able to crack) published earlier this very year.

Yes, *published.*

Because, you see, our lawyer, asbestos manufacturer, and canny investor in the Habsburg Empire's future is also a writer in his spare time. And not just like the countless young men who try their hand at writing these days (so many that German has coined the word *Primanerdrama*—"the sort of play written by a high school student"). No, he's a real, commercially published writer. However much Mom and his ex-fiancée wish it were true, writing is not just a hobby, or an "interest" (God, he hates that word!) with him. To him, it's his *real life.* And just three weeks ago, he found out that he has been given the sort of career-making break that most authors can only dream of . . .

In Which Our Hero Almost Cracks Berlin, Is Knocked Back, Then Has Good Reason to Be Glad He Is Friendly with a Certain Dr. Franz Blei

Not that he's exactly been unlucky so far. How many authors get drawn to the public's attention before they have brought out a single word anywhere?

Well, early in 1907, our lawyer's best friend Max Brod (a classic literary networker with fingers in many bookish pies) did just that for him. While writing a Berlin book review of a novel by one Franz Blei, he named our man as a great stylist, right there alongside several already famous writers. Quite a plug for an entirely unpublished man!

It was a whole year before readers could check out Max's claims for themselves: in early 1908 and again in 1909, our hero's first short pieces appeared in a short-lived but very upscale literary journal called *Hyperion,* edited by a good friend of Max's, a publisher, translator, dandy, and general literary operator of astounding energy who zips back and forth between the avant-garde literary circles of Berlin, Prague, and Vienna—Franz Blei again, in fact.

Hyperion was a very good place indeed for a new author to be seen. No obscure journal, this: the millionaire playwright Carl Sternheim backed it financially and lent it his coeditorial respectability. Lavishly produced in the latest style, it attracted such big names as Rainer Maria Rilke and Heinrich Mann. Our hero's tidbits were impressive enough—and fitted into a recognizable enough modern style—for many people to assume that they'd been written under a pseudonym by the established author Robert Walser.

Since then, he's published a few other small things in the papers, a short story he regards as his breakthrough work and two small (but undeniable) books. Famous he may not yet be, but the big trade advertisement in early 1913 for his first book, *Meditation* (a collection of those short magazine pieces and some fragments from an unfinished work), already felt able to declare confidently that he "has long been known to those who follow the development of our best young writers . . . a writer and a book arousing great interest from every side." The second book, also released in 1913, was actually the stand-alone first chapter of a novel he has never managed to crack, and was very well reviewed by the up-and-coming Robert Musil, among others.

In fact, Musil liked his stuff so much that, last spring, he invited him to jump ship from the new Leipzig house of Kurt Wolff & Co. (who have given him his early breaks) to the highly established Fischer of Berlin.

He was tempted, and let Musil come to pick up his latest novella. It was a little bit unfair to Kurt Wolff, perhaps, who had already heard of this new story through Max's carefully managed grapevine, had asked to see it and had even discussed publication. But, well, after all, Fischer is *the* Berlin publisher, and our hero and Wolff have yet to formally agree on publication, so . . . *

There were also broad hints that Musil could fix up some kind of regular income for him, writing for the most prestigious German-language cultural journal, Fischer's *New Review,* which our hero has read for over a decade and which Musil now edits. No one likes to talk openly to artistic colleagues about money and jobs, of course, but Musil invited him in writing to consider the *New Review* as "your personal mouthpiece," which was pretty clear. Think of it: paid work at the heart of Berlin's electric literary scene! On

---

*Reiner Stach thinks he may have been *deliberately* holding out on Wolff in order to wriggle out of an option on his next work, thus keeping the new story free to front up his longed-for assault on literary Berlin. No one will ever know, but such contracts were common at the time (the hero of Evelyn Waugh's *Vile Bodies* is trapped in just this way) and it's certainly striking that after telling Wolff in 1913 that it just wasn't ready, our hero straight away showed the same version to Musil when *he* asked in 1914

April 18, 1914, our hero proudly announced that the *New Review* was taking the story and making him "other charming offers."*

Then disaster struck. Samuel Fischer personally insisted, over Robert Musil's head, that they would have to cut the story substantially for publication. Cut it? After all that careful work? Cut the longest thing he had ever considered to be finished? If Musil can't even deliver on a promised publication, what are his other "charming offers" worth?

Our hero went back to Kurt Wolff, asking very politely but forthrightly for a decision about his publication. As a result, the story has just come out in the October edition of Wolff & Co.'s flagship literary journal, the achingly trendy *White Pages.*

Then, on October 11, just three weeks ago, the very day on which Bulgaria decided that the Germans and Austro-Hungarians were now certain to win the war, something else interesting happened: Wolff & Co. wrote to him that they wanted to bring out the new story in a proper book version as well—and fast—in their top-of-the-line series, *The Day of Judgment.*

Why this sudden enthusiasm? Well, actually, the fact is that there have been some rather interesting behind-the-scenes machinations concerning Berlin's prestigious Fontane Prize (named in honor of the greatest recent German novelist). The sort of thing the reading public, bless it, really doesn't need to know about.

This year, 1915, the Fontane Prize judge is . . . Franz Blei.

Indeed. The Franz Blei whose novel *The Dark Path* provided the excuse for Brod to plug our then as-yet-unpublished hero. The Franz Blei whose *Hyperion* was the first journal ever to publish his work. The Franz Blei with whom he and Brod walked out to see Halley's Comet on the night it approached most closely to the Earth in 1910. The Franz Blei whose operetta collaboration with Brod he was

---

*He didn't announce this fine news to his fiancée but to her younger, prettier best friend, whom he was at the time lining up in the expectation that his engagement would shortly be called off. As we'll see later.

discussing on the evening in 1912 when he met Miss Felice Bauer. The Franz Blei who contributed to the yearbook (*Arcadia*) in which Brod published "The Judgment." Our hero had even reviewed Blei's own work in a Berlin journal (warmly, of course: he wrote to Blei personally, apologizing for some misprints). When *Hyperion* closed down in 1911, he wrote an appreciation of it in Cousin Bruno's paper *Bohemia*. In this article, our hero doesn't spare careful criticism, showing his knowledge of German literary currents and even of practical "gaps" (his word) in the publishing market—but he called Blei "this admirable man," saying that "certainly no journal has ever erred more nobly" and foretold that once the dust has settled, *Hyperion* would become "a bibliophile treasure."

Yes, all in all, our hero is very well known to the man who is not only the judge of the Fontane Prize this year, but also happens to be the founder (and until recently, the editor) of the very literary magazine—Wolff's *White Pages*—in which his striking new novella has just now appeared.

Small world, the literary one.

However, in awarding the 1915 Fontane Prize, Blei has not gone daringly for one of his young friends and protégés. Like so many literary prize judges, he has opted for a safe choice, a writer no one can possibly object to. And the winner is . . . Carl Sternheim.

Yes, Sternheim. The same man who so generously helped out Blei's *Hyperion* with his name and his money in 1908. Whose hit comedy *The Knickers* featured Blei himself in a small part at its premiere in 1911.* And who is, by another happy coincidence, now also published by Kurt Wolff & Co.

But wait, there's a problem! Carl Sternheim is not just Germany's most famous playwright, he is also extremely well off, having been born rich and married much richer. Think about it: no

---

*It's still a standard in the German theater and was produced in Los Angeles by Hollywood star Steve Martin, starring himself, in 2004.

one can begrudge a Carl Sternheim the laurels of a literary prize, but one can hardly expect a gentleman writer of such distinction and wealth, who lives in a vast country house on his own estate, to publicly hold out his hand and thank you for a check, like some butler accepting a tip! The thing is clearly just not possible.

What to do?

Well, clever Dr. Blei has come up with a crafty and unusual (and rather newsworthy) solution to his own problem. His rich friend and sometime patron Sternheim will accept the actual *prize*—but will grandly and publicly insist that the *money* goes to a junior writer, "as a sign of his recognition."

And who might that lucky young writer be?

Why, who else but good friend Max's best friend?

What a well-spun boost for a fledgling author everyone likes. And what fine advertising copy, by the by, for Franz Blei's regular employers, Kurt Wolff & Co., who publish both him and Sternheim. As for the ordinary book-buying public, well, they don't need to know all the boring backstage details, do they? Of course not. When did they ever . . . ?*

In Which Our Hero Gets Some Very Good News, Gets on a Rather High Horse, and Then Gets off Again

The elegant Herr Kurt Wolff himself having been called away on pressing business at the Western Front, it was his business manager, Herr G. H. Meyer, a man who had already shown a good nose for the modern book market, who broke this excellent (and as yet secret) news to our hero on October 11.

---

*At my first publishing party, the wonderful novelist Howard Jacobson took me under his wing: "I suppose", said he, "that being new to this game you think the book world is run by a bunch of well-off metropolitan authors who plug each other all the time in the press?" Not wanting to seem a callow and envious provincial, I laughed: "Oh no, I'm sure it doesn't *really* work like that." "Well of course it does", he pointed to a group in the corner, "and there they are."

His jolly letter stressed how much publicity the Fontane Prize affair would get; it explained that this made it highly desirable from Wolff & Co.'s point of view to bring out a book version of the novella quickly (and to reissue our hero's first little book); it totalled up the monies now awaiting the young writer from the prize and from his advances.

Good Herr Meyer no doubt expected a grateful reply from his author, who was surely clever enough to realize how much this behind-the-scenes coup could mean to his literary prospects. A major prize half-awarded not just from little Prague, not even from Vienna, but from Berlin, the capital of Germany (and German writing) itself! With the public blessing of Germany's best-known playwright, the great Sternheim!

The actual reply must have made Herr Meyer blink.

True, perhaps it was a little tactless of Herr Meyer to admit so candidly that this sudden publicity was the reason Wolff & Co. wanted to bring out the book. Arguably, it was a bit heavy handed to add up the money like that and talk about the new prices of our hero's books, as if mere money is what writing and publishing are all about.

It was quite a decent sum, though. The Fontane Prize purse alone would cover three whole months full board at the famous and fashionable (and nudist) Jungborn Sanatorium, which our hero had so enjoyed in 1912. And anyway, look, our man's a big-city lawyer who knows who's who and what's what, not some innocent poet from the countryside, isn't he?

Well, yes, maybe it *was* a tad too familiar to call him "a real Lucky Jim."* But Herr Wolff always sensed what a modest and quiet fellow this author is: when they were introduced (by Max, who else, who presented him to Wolff "like an impresario bringing on his star act") the allegedly up-and-coming genius,

---

*Meyer actually wrote that our hero was a "Hans im Glück" ("a happy Hans").

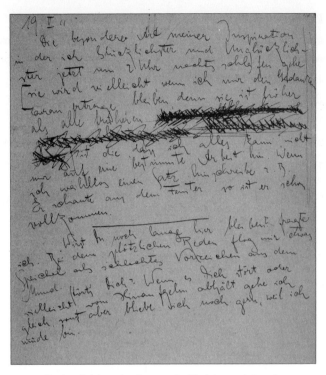

Our hero's internal policeman double-takes and steps in.

thirty next birthday, had sat there as shyly as a schoolboy at an exam.

Grateful? Of course he should be.

Little do either Meyer or Wolff know that this publicly self-effacing man has a somewhat different side to him. But then again, no one knows this, not even Max. There is, for example, a certain famous poetess who remembers our handsome hero as almost saintly after spending an evening out with him and the gang in Berlin—and who would doubtless be surprised to know that he actually thinks of her as little more than a drunk staggering from bar to bar.[7]

Ever polite in public, he's quite capable of privately bad-mouthing even the biggest living writers (he's particularly scathing about the recent work of Vienna's leading literary lion, Arthur

Schnitzler). Back in February 1911, when he had only ever published a few magazine pieces and a couple of reviews, he had written in his secret diary that "in intellectual/spiritual matters there is no doubt that I am now the focal point of Prague." Having evidently taken himself by surprise, he obliterated the phrase with deep pen strokes.*

But Herr Meyer naturally had no idea of all this, so when he received his reply, it must have made him stare in disbelief.

Gratitude? Modesty? Shyness? Not quite.

The letter was a masterpiece of cold irony, steel and pride glinting through every sentence. It contained lawyerly reminders about what Herr Wolff had agreed to verbally in the past (conveniently ignoring the fact that, in the meantime, our hero had tried to place the story somewhere else).† While accepting the company's hiked-up plans for his works, the letter attempted to push them even further, to revive his other book to ride on the back of this new success. It was all topped off by nit-picking authorial jealousy of the layout of *Napoleon* (by his condescending would-be benefactor, Carl Sternheim).

In fact, almost the only thing this "happy Hans" *did* accept without demur was that the publicity would do him good.

15 October 1915

Dear Herr Meyer,

Many thanks for your letter of the 11th. Your news, especially concerning Blei and Sternheim, gave me great pleasure—and in many

---

*He wrote "im Geistigen"—a mixture of "intellectual" and "spiritual" for which (perhaps luckily) English has no translation. Seventy years later, a zealous researcher, treating his diary as one might an ancient parchment, revealed what had been so carefully (but not carefully enough) deleted. Paper, it turns out, is as hard to clean as windows.

†He will repeatedly refer to Wolff's verbal promise next year, when (successfully) campaigning to have *The Judgment* brought out as a stand-alone book.

ways. As far as your actual questions regarding *The Metamorphosis* go (though they weren't genuine questions, since it is in fact already typeset) I would be able to give my firm opinion if I knew how things stood with the Fontane Prize. I gather from your letter, and above all from having written to Max Brod, that things seem to be as follows: Sternheim gets the prize, but hands the money on to someone else, possibly me. Although this is all very charming, it implies that the question being asked is one of need—not of need for the prize and the money, but simply of need for the money. And in that case my feeling is that this could not be a question of who might possibly need the money one day in the future: it would simply have to be decided on the basis of who needs it right now. As important as the prize, or a share of the prize, would be to me, I see no way in which I could accept the money on its own without any share at all in the prize itself. I would have no right to do so, since I myself am certainly not at present in that requisite state of financial necessity. The one section of your letter that argues against my position is where you write that "thanks to the Fontane Prize, the public's attention etc." At any rate, the whole business remains uncertain and I would be very thankful for a little clarification.

As for your suggestions, I entrust myself completely to you. It would have actually been my wish to bring out a larger book of novellas (e.g., the novella from *Arkadia*, *The Metamorphosis*, and another novella, under the joint title *Punishments*) and Herr Wolff did once earlier agree to this, but under the present circumstances your proposal is no doubt better. I am also completely in agreement with the new edition of *Meditation*.

I enclose the galley proofs of *The Metamorphosis*. It pains me that you have used a different typeface from that in *Napoleon* despite the fact that I could interpret your having sent *Napoleon* to me as a promise that *The Metamorphosis* would be printed in the same type. As it is, the layout of *Napoleon* is bright and easy on the eye, while that of *The Metamorphosis* is dark and crowded (though the font size is, I think, the same). If this can still be changed, it would be very much in accordance with my wishes.

I don't know how the later volumes in the *Day of Judgment* series were bound, but "The Stoker" was not attractive. It was done in some kind of imitation stuff and, after a while at least, one could hardly bear to look at it. I would therefore ask for a new edition.

What a pity you could not come last week. Perhaps it will be possible soon. I would be very glad.

Our hero, so bold on paper, evidently thinks again about getting onto so high a horse in reality, for in his very next letter to Herr Meyer, five days later, he reports that although the whole business of the Fontane Prize is still "unclear" to him, and he still bemoans the fact that it's "only and exclusively" a question of the money, not the actual prize, he has indeed written to thank Sternheim—stressing, however, that he did so only on Wolff & Co.'s advice and complaining, "It is rather hard to write to someone from whom one has had no direct communication and to thank him without knowing quite what for."

He also includes (unrequested) a package of his reviews to date, noting that it was "sent to him" as complete, but listing several gaps.* He helpfully points out to Herr Meyer those that are "the most important" (the one by Robert Musil) and "the most positive."

Finally, he checks that Meyer has received another piece intended for an anthology—it's the little fable called "Before the Law" that was first published in a Zionist newspaper earlier this year—and asks (rather ingenuously, perhaps) for Franz Blei's address, so that he can thank him as well.

---

*Who sent our hero this allegedly complete set of his reviews? Stach thinks he must have employed a cuttings-agency.

A major literary-prize winner with great reviews.

So writerly pride is swallowed, the behind-the-scenes plan is put into action, the prize is awarded to the great Sternheim, the money is passed on with a public flourish to the junior writer of his choice—and an advertisement comes out, making good use of those reviews. The reviews excerpted for the ad are pretty hot (the publishers, as publishers will, make their own selection). Any writer would be glad of them, especially one who doesn't actually live in either of the capitals of the German language:

> I can easily imagine someone into whose hand this book falls finding that their whole life is altered from this hour onward, that they become a new person.
> —*März* (Munich)

A remarkably great, remarkably fine book by a gentle genius of a writer!

—*Daily News* (Berlin)

Events are described with such purity of style, such charming cadences, with such precision and maturity, that one can only make comparison with classics of literature. —*New Free Press* (Vienna)

Over these fifty pages there lies a unique glow, as of high summer. Nothing is beside the point, there is not a sentence, hardly even a word, that stands in shadow. —*The National News* (Berlin)

It's hard to describe a book that has just left you feeling as though you've experienced a miracle. —*Germany on Monday* (Berlin)

Fine stuff. Conceivably, though, the book-buying public might have been interested to know exactly *who* wrote these splendid reviews. The first is by our hero's best friend, Max Brod; the second by Albert Ehrenstein (with whom he is friendly enough to be have been photographed messing about in the mock-up plane in Vienna two years ago); the third by Camill Hoffmann, a Prague poet and editor who knows Brod well;* the fourth by our hero's second-best friend (and closest confidant at the time of the breakup of his engagement last year), Ernst Weiss; and the last by Heinrich Eduard Jacob, who also contributed to the yearbook *Arcadia* (ed. Max Brod) in which our hero's first major story was published.

In other words, it's frankly arguable whether a single one of these fine reviews can truly be called neutral or objective. But who ever bothered telling outsiders that kind of thing?†

---

*And who, in 1933, as Czech cultural attaché in Berlin, will vainly try to get back from the Gestapo the boxes confiscated from our hero's last fiancée's flat.

†I'm not suggesting that these men lied for him. Few reviewers will actually puff something that's no good (the blatant pulling and sweetening of punches where well-connected or untouchably established writers are concerned is quite another matter). Being good is generally a *necessary* condition of getting well reviewed—but by no means always a *sufficient* one. As in every walk of life, you have to be good *and* lucky. This is where friends in the right places come in very handy—and our hero clearly has plenty of them.

When the ads come out, his ex-fiancée in Berlin notes his new success. Our hero, on this occasion distinctly economical with the truth while perhaps just about skirting around outright lies (ah, lawyers!) explains to her that he "almost" found out about the Fontane Prize first from the press, that his publisher had "only once vaguely prepared him for the news" and that he knows Sternheim "neither personally nor as a writer."

In Which Our Hero Squeezes His Handkerchief Rhythmically by Way of Stress Relief

Well, however it happened, it happened, and there it is in black and white for all to see forever. One way or another, things are looking up for our hero's literary career and, by the sound of things, he knows it quite well, thank you very much.

Which means he really hasn't got any excuse any longer. He's been going on for years about making the break, leaving Prague, trying to earn a living by writing alone. Of course, that's a massive step: Max (who's a far better-known writer than he is) still can't do without a day job. Who wouldn't be wary of making the jump from one's home town, one's circle of supportive friends, and one's totally secure, well-paid career, without some pretty definite evidence that one will get a welcome (and be able to make a living) in the Big City?

But now he'd be going to Berlin (where else *is* there for an ambitious young German author?) with half the Fontane Prize in his back pocket, very good connections, and two almost-completed novels in his suitcase.

He was working hard on both novels this time last year and—who knows?—if he's free of the office, perhaps he'll be able to find the concentrated time to finish them at last. He's already happy with a central little part of the newer one (that fable he just sent to

Herr Meyer). When he read the start of the novel to Max and some other friends, he had the whole roomful of them (as well as himself) "laughing helplessly" at the arrest of a certain Josef K.[8] He's also got that striking short story (it's called "In the Penal Colony") that he wanted Wolff & Co. to include in an anthology, which he feels just needs the end reworked.*

Not a bad top drawer to go with. And he figures he's got two years' grace. He can afford to live for that long even if he can't earn a penny from his literary work at first, because he's got well over a year's salary carefully stashed away in the bank for this very purpose (thanks largely to having lived rent-free off his parents for so long).

That's settled then: he'll do it! He'll make himself take the leap to that point where there's no going back—surely, that's the only way to live? He'll leave his home town, his family, his job, just as he had decided to last summer.

But it'll have to wait until after the war, naturally. He physically, legally, can't go now—how could he? But the end looks to be within sight. Which brings him back outside the door of the war bond outlet once again. *5.5 percent tax-free!* Now, if he put his nest egg into those bonds, it could really help his new life, when peace returns. It's really just question of how many to buy.

He goes to the shop twice, and walks away twice. He feverishly totals up the interest. He runs back home and asks his mother to buy the bonds for him. Then he doubles the amount he first thought of. This means that he now plans to invest an amount equal to over a third of his newly increased annual salary. He is surprised to find that there already is a war bond for more than that in his own name, of which he knew nothing—it must have been made using the money he thought he'd invested in the

---

*It involves a curious machine that writes laws into people's bodies rather like his ex-fiancée's dictation-machines write into wax cylinders.

asbestos factory.[9] The news hardly affects him. He's filled with thoughts of his new investment. He worries about it: even a half-hour's walk through the liveliest streets of Prague doesn't clear his head. He mulls over the figures, considers the general financial climate, and recalculates the amounts of interest that will one day be his to dispose of as he thinks fit. As he strides, his excitement gradually transforms and his thoughts redirect themselves to his writing. He feels that he is capable of it, he wants nothing except the possibility of writing, he works out which of the following nights he'll be able to devote to it, and races, his heart aching, over the stone bridge, feeling as so often before, the unhappiness of the devouring fire that cannot be allowed to break out. To calm himself and let it out, he invents a saying, "Little friend, pour forth yourself," which he sings incessantly to a certain tune, accompanying himself by squeezing and letting go the handkerchief in his pocket over and over again, as if it were a bagpipe . . . *

*This entire paragraph is directly taken from the diary entry of 5th November 1915. It's hard to believe our hero didn't know *exactly* what he was writing at the end. He really does seem to have thought of writing almost literally as a sexual act. After all, he told Brod straight out that when setting down the final sentence of *The Judgment* (the last word of which is a clear multiple-entendre in German) he'd been thinking of "a strong ejaculation."

II

INTO THE LOCKED BOOKCASE

A 1913 advertisement for one of the clubs where Kafka
suggested taking a special early breakfast.

This, then, is how that wonderful black comedy *The Metamorphosis*, the most famous short story of the twentieth century—arguably, its most famous single literary work, period—came to be published when, where, and how it did.[1]

Sorry, comedy?

Well, I'd like to know how else we're supposed to read a story in which a man changes into a beetle while sleeping; realizes that it's no dream; tries to go back to sleep but fails, due to nothing more profound than now being unable to turn over onto his side; and then (rather than letting out a primal scream of terror), thinks: "Oh God, why did I have to choose such a stressful job? On the road, day after day." Black, yes, but comedy, surely.

Of course, we're not used to seeing *The Metamorphosis* as a comedy of any kind. But then again, we're not used to seeing that this amazing story *didn't* slip out into the world as some unnoticed, underground work by an obscure man, only to be discovered after his lonely death (and so on). We're unused to seeing that it was written

by man who'd for several years been published in good places with
the backing of a powerful, cutting-edge literary clique and that, after the author had rather sneakily tried to place it with a rival (and
more important) publisher, it was eventually launched off the back
of an insider publicity coup with a fanfare that may seem modest
by today's standards but was about as loud as book advertising got
in 1915.

The reason we're not used to seeing things this way is very
simple: No one has ever really come clean about it.

In fact, the standard English-language biographies scarcely
even mention the Fontane Prize business at all: Hayman only
notes it in his chronological table (where he gets the year wrong)
and Pawel gives the affair one short paragraph, saying that Kafka
was "baffled" by this "gesture."

Well, we've now seen Kafka's whole letter on the subject, uncut for once, for ourselves: I suggest that "baffled" is not *quite* the
right word for his state of mind there.

The whole thing is astonishing, really. Kafka was a *writer*, for
God's sake. That's, in the end, the only reason we care about anything else in his life (hard though it is to recall this amid the biographical tumult of the tourist guides and academic conferences).
And in the life of a writer, publicly half-winning a pretty major
literary prize is rather an important event, surely?

His contemporaries were in no doubt of it: when he was invited to read his work in Munich almost exactly a year later, the
organizers released a press announcement on November 9, the day
before the event, describing him simply as

Franz Kafka, the writer to whom the Fontane Prize was handed
last year

It seems that the K.-myth is the problem here. Perhaps Kafka's
biographers simply don't *like* the idea that their literary idol was

helped out in this very earthly (and arguably even somewhat underhanded) way in the vital early stages of his career.

And certainly, no one has ever admitted another nonsecret: that the great Dr. Franz Kafka and the frankly rather dubious Dr. Franz Blei actually go back even further than we've seen, and rather more murkily.

They go back, in fact, right into Kafka's locked bookcase . . .

A Notebook Bill Gates Couldn't Buy

Before we look back almost exactly a century, into that locked bookcase, remember: Kafka is now a vast academic and publishing (and tourist) industry. Of all the authors in all the world, only Shakespeare generates more Ph.D.s, more biographies, more coffee-table books, and more trinkets than Kafka does.

Everything Kafka wrote, every postcard he ever sent, every page of his diary, every business memorandum he ever dictated, is regarded as a potential Arc of the Covenant that may be handled only by Top People. If you were in a junk shop in Berlin and happened across (say) an authentic twenty-word postcard from Dr. Franz Kafka to Miss Felice Bauer, dated any time between September 1912 and December 1917, you could confidently order a modest new Mercedes on the spot. If it was dated any later, make that a fully equipped Bentley. If you were camping in an old barn in the former East Germany and found one of the boxes of stuff the Gestapo took from Kafka's last love's flat, and in it found a notebook in Kafka's writing, your children's children would bless the day as they sipped cocktails on their own private airplane.

There are many notebooks like this at Oxford University, thanks to the dedication of the late, great Sir Malcolm Pasley and the generosity of Kafka's descendant, Marianne Steiner. In the early eighties I was once, by sheer and absurd fluke, allowed to

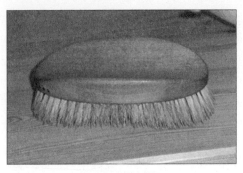

The Holy Hairbrush.

hold one of the books. I've never forgotten the impact of the sheer *ordinariness*. These were once just notebooks, written in by a human being. Now, their worth is anyone's guess. One estimate in the 1990s put the value of the university's Kafka Collection at £100,000,000.[2] That's entirely meaningless because Oxford will never, ever sell them, to anyone, for anything, any more than the Louvre would or could sell the *Mona Lisa*. For once, *priceless* is exactly the right word, because Kafka's originals are now quite literally beyond monetary value. There are not many things that Bill Gates couldn't buy, but Kafka's little notebooks are among them. Top academics will line up for years—maybe forever—to examine these volumes: you or I would have as much chance of getting to stroke them now as we would of being allowed to kiss the Turin Shroud.

In the 1990s, a mighty argument broke out about who had the right to work directly from the original manuscripts now that Kafka was dead long enough to be coming out of copyright. Eminent professors from Germany and Oxford and Yale accused one another in the newspapers and on TV of breaking the rules of scholarship or even the law, of only being in it for the money, of being crypto-Communists, and worse. Sir Malcolm's German rivals insisted on calling him *Sir Pasley* in their public fulminations, thus relegating themselves, in the ears of all English-speakers, to agreeably farcical Teutonic stereotypes. Kafka is so important that even the German ambassador to London became involved.

The *German* ambassador? But surely Kafka was *Czech*? Well, we'll see about that later, too. At any rate, so legendary has Kafka become that when his elegant, military-style English hairbrush (the only known physical artifact accepted to have been in holy contact with his living body) was discovered in Israel, it made the world news.

The scholar who can decipher one erased line of Kafka's diary, or prove that his rivals have all gotten wrong the hotel he went to on such and such a day in 1913, will be quoted in theses forever.

Yet *no one* has ever shown his readers what we are about to see: Kafka's porn.

Finding Kafka's Porn

When I began this book I had no idea about Kafka's porn for the simple reason that no one has ever discussed it, let alone published it, in any essay, article, or book an Kafka.

I'd just read, in Peter-André Alt's great biography of him, that Kafka deeply admired (and early on, even imitated) the poetry of Stefan George. Because I knew George was openly antidemocratic (not to mention, almost openly pederastic), wrote in sonorous cadences, and practiced a high-priest-of-art shtick, I'd never even thought of putting him together with Kafka (I was too in thrall to the K.-myth for that). So I looked closely at this section of the biography.

Alt mentions George's special custom typeface. This made me think of the extra-big typeface used for Kafka's first little book and how not being able to get the right typeface delayed publication of "A Country Doctor" and generally how Kafka worried about what his writing would actually, physically *look* like in print.

When I idly Googled up stuff about pre–Great War German

typefaces (sometimes you need to listen to your inner geek), I found the name of the man who had cut Stefan George's special typeface. I checked him out, and the first link I found was to the Berlin Gay Museum, which had placed online a newly acquired picture by him. I thought I recognized the named source of this picture as the "journal of unusual art and literature" that Kafka owned.

So, of course, I looked.

The Top Shelf of the Bodleian Library,
or the Mystery of the Nonsecret

Kafka's porn is no real secret. The mystery is that it should seem like one. Like the Fontane Prize business, it's been known about (or rather, know*able* about) since Kafka's very first biography. Max Brod, Kafka's best friend and step-author of his novels, included a tactful footnote identifying a "periodical to which we subscribed together." Most decent-size modern volumes on Kafka's life have briefly noted this, and since Wagenbach published his epochal *Kafka: A Biography of His Youth* in 1958, everyone who wants to has been able to know what sort of "periodical" this really was.

What's more, it's not just easy to find out *that* Kafka owned porn, it's even easy to *find* the stuff, either in the efficient, modern British Library in London or the splendid, timeless Bodleian Library in Oxford.

This is, thanks to Sir Malcolm's matchless collection, the natural home of world Kafka studies. Every year, scores of fresh, eager Kafka students from all corners of the earth enter that library in Oxford, clever young people in zealous pursuit of grades or the grail, postgraduates who have devoted their irreplaceable twenties to yet more years of Kafka, tenure-track professors seeking the insights that will ensure their pension rights. And all of them sit there, noting little details about his work, his engagements, his reading, his family, his

friends, his beliefs, staring for hours at screens showing digital fac-
similes of the untouchable original manuscripts, as if any of these
might provide the golden key to unlock his work—when, all the
while, what Kafka liked to look at in private is lying a mere few
yards away, all but ignored by two entire scholarly generations. I sat
down there myself a hundred times in the 1980s, little knowing.

The whole business is frankly bizarre. At first I tried to explain
it to myself by little theories about the difference between words
and pictures. Are scholars, obsessed with "acts of writing" (as they
put it), just not mentally able to discuss pornographic drawings?
Are pictures somehow too telling, too dangerous, too direct?
Kafka has become a vast academic industry: to use a ghastly German word for a ghastly worldwide thing, he has been officially declared *theoriefähig*—"fit for theorizing about." Is his collection of
porn too simple and basic a witness, one that can't be reduced to
yet more job-creating word-games about *hermeneutics, intertextual-
ity, deconstruction* and so on?* After all, we are supposed to be interested in this man's mental world, his psyche, his feelings, aren't
we? Maybe looking at his porn is as misleading for academics of
the written word as examining the films he loved—films that, unlike real experiences, could easily make him cry?

But I think it's actually far simpler than that. The distinguished
editors of the standard modern German reference work, *Franz Kafka:
Eine Chronik* (Wagenbach, 1999), for whom generally no event in
Kafka's life is too banal to investigate, certainly maintain the cover-
up about his porn (they merely note that he subscribed to a "bibliophile quarterly")—but they are just as coy about the diaries. When
they say that Kafka spoke to Brod about his "existential fears" on
January 23, 1922 (just before he began *The Castle*) they give no hint
that the actual subject of the conversation, which Brod found
"moved me deeply," was Kafka's compulsive visit to a brothel.

---

*Students of Kafka (or of anything else) should note that the more jargon a tutor uses, the less
they're worth listening to.

The plain fact seems to be that scholars just don't *want* to know—which, they being the gatekeepers of the facts, means that they don't want *you*, dear Reader, to know—about the real Franz Kafka, warts, porn, whores, and all. The effect is one of censorship pure and simple. So it seems high time that we at last unlocked that long-sealed bookcase . . .

Into the Locked Bookcase

In 1906, Dr. Franz Blei, future hander-out of the Fontane Prize, published a journal called *The Amethyst* in a strictly limited edition for pre-paid subscribers only.

The Amethyst was officially banned when a salesman from Breslau (whom Blei evidently thought was a police stooge) lodged an official complaint at supposedly having found a copy lying in his hotel room.* This allowed the Viennese authorities to claim that *The Amethyst* was in "general circulation" and thus to shut it down on moral grounds because of the illustrations. Blei thereupon changed the title to *Opals* for 1907, which fooled no one except the imperial censors.

The pictures in *The Amethyst/Opals* are nestled within many, many more pages of words. Some of these words are nothing whatever to do with sex—translations of Keats, for example. Some are a bit radical or daring (such as versions of Verlaine or excerpts from the diaries of Wilde's notorious collaborator, Aubrey Beardsley), but no more than that.

There's also edgy fiction by young-gun authors—among it (as he omits to mention) are several of Max Brod's very own productions: spicy love poems; a "sketched novel" called *The Whim of Eros*, in which a man manages, Restoration comedy–style, to have his cake

---

*The Habsburg police maintained an army of informers. This will be important to recall.

(in the curvaceous shape of an ever-willing blond wench) and eat it (in the form of his middle-class soul mate); and a soft-porn romance "The Czech Serving-Girl," whose blond-braided, "porcelain"-breasted, baby-talking heroine, Pepi, takes our German hero to places he has never been, literally and metaphorically.*

The pictures in *The Amethyst/Opals* are massively outnumbered by the words. When one flips the pages idly, the illustrations seem to be just another part of the whole magazine—which is, of course, exactly the impression that upscale pornographers *do* want to give, be it *Opals* in 1907 or *Penthouse* in 2007.

And in any case, a good deal of the writing here *is* porn, and the careful framing devices are part of it. Descriptions of sex are set up as stories "from the Hindustani" or as cod-classical smoking-room debates about "the psychology of the courtesan" and so on. These devices may seem arch to us now, but they were as familiar to Edwardian aficionados as the alleged "reader's letter" is to modern pornographers.†

As a maker of upscale porn, Dr. Blei knows that the nonporn, soft-porn, and lit-porn content is a vital part of selling his wares. Having plenty of this stuff around allows men to kid themselves that they are buying "slick, highbrow magazines" that just happen to include "exotic erotica" (this is how Pawel's biography describes them).

In January 1922, Kafka's diary notes that he's always tried to delude his own conscience using just this side step concerning his compulsive visits to prostitutes: he's "always and everywhere," says he, tried to arrange these things so that they could feel like spontaneous "opportunities," not planned undertakings.

In reality, of course, there is nothing tangential about the pic-

---

Pepi is the top porn-name of the day, the name of the underage heroine in the still-shocking, still-in-print 1906 Viennese bestseller *Josefine Mutzenbacher*. It's unlikely that Kafka didn't recall this when he came to name the little blond maid who, sixteen years on, offers herself to K. in *The Castle*.

†For example, to bring up Plato's *Symposium* in conversation (never mind, throughout *Death in Venice*) was an Edwardian code that showed you were (a) posh and (b) potentially gay.

LE GOURMAND

tures in *The Amethyst/Opals* (or *Penthouse*) at all. The pages and pages of cool debates, lush poems, racy modern prose, erotic tales, and uncut classics are merely the first coy layers of a striptease whose climax materially involves the illustrations for which men *really* ordered (and paid for) these pricey journals in advance.

Some of Dr. Blei's porn seems rather gay, such as the one above. Some of it, like the one on page 63, seems rather Victorian.

And the one on page 64 looks rather surprisingly like *Barbarella* or something else from the bold 1960s (apart from the pantaloons, obviously).*

---

*Making you wonder if historians of the future will say that sixty years of war, revolution and horror, cold and hot, between Expressionist 1908 and Hippie 1968 simply put things briefly on hold . . .

For the avoidance of doubt, as the lawyers say, it's certain that Kafka personally owned this particular pornography—and that he did *not* do so by chance or simply on a passing whim.

He was an enthusiastic subscriber to both incarnations of the magazine: "What's going on with *The Amethyst?*" he wrote to Brod on February 2, 1906, "My money is ready and waiting"; in August 1907, he took his *Opals* on a vacation where he did lots of motorbike riding, drank lots of beer, and was up in the park until midnight with "a burdensomely infatuated girl"; on October 10, 1907, he

complained that the new issue of *Opals* had been delayed—"Why is God punishing Blei, Germany, and us? And especially me?" he mock-bewailed.

This wasn't in some period of teenage or student prankery. At this time, he had already written his first known extended attempt at fiction ("Description of a Struggle," 1904/5). He was producing short pieces like the wonderful "The Refusal," which he was happy to publish later, and embarking on "Wedding Preparations in the Country." In other words, Kafka was buying and reading *The Amethyst/Opals* while writing things that are still quite rightly studied around the world as part of his work proper. Indeed, he had already had his first glowing mention in the literary press—although this was, as we've seen, somewhat unusually, before he had published a single word.

Kafka kept his collection of *The Amethyst/Opals* at home at his parents' place, in a locked bookcase. He took the key away with him in August 1907 when he left the apartment to go on vacation, taking the new *Opals* but leaving last year's *Amethyst* safely tucked away. In the same locked bookcase, he kept a bankbook from a secret savings account that he didn't want to be found because "to me it decides my rank in the family." He assumed (correctly) that his erotic secrets were safe in this bookcase. The stellar Viennese playwright of the day, Arthur Schnitzler, was not so lucky. *His* papa invoked the supposed rights of a Victorian father and householder to break into a son's locked desk, thus discovering young Schnitzler's diary of his jolly whoring. The experience permanently scarred relationships between them.*

Kafka's locked bookcase in his parents' apartment—his one private space within the bustle of his family, the storehouse of his secret writings, his secret money, his secret porn—is a gorgeous image. It sets off echoes throughout his writing: unspoken and guilt-edged sexual desire, family power play, secret doors, cupboards, and locks (the German for "lock"—*Schloss*—is also the German for "castle"). Not to mention, the inherent dubiousness of a life devoted to solitary quests and pursuits such as, well, literature . . .

As we'll see on the following pages, he did well to keep his porn locked away, because it really *isn't* the sort of stuff you'd want

---

*It'll be worth remembering that the monstrous Hermann Kafka, unlike the renowned Professor Schnitzler, respected his son's privacy.

You're not a woman to me, you're a girl, I've never seen anyone more girlish,
there's no way I'll dare to hold out my hand to you, girl, my dirty,
twitching, clawlike, nervous, uncertain, hot-cold hand.
—Letter to Milena, June 12, 1920

Mother (who'd be weepily distressed) or Father (who'd roar with
delighted scorn) or your admiring little sisters (with whom you
feel freer and more confident than with anyone else) to find lying
about the place. I mean, sex is sex, but some of the pictures are a
little bit bizarre, such as the one on the opposite page.

And some of them, such as the one above, are quite frankly,
well, rather *dark* . . .

Or even scary. On page 68 is the actual picture quoted by the
authorities when banning *The Amethyst* and, although Blei, like an
Edwardian Larry Flynt, mocked them for saying it was immoral,
you have to say they do have a point.

This was not the only "unusual literature" Kafka read and
owned in the formative years of his midtwenties. He bought
the notorious modern Sade disciple Octave Mirbeau's *Sin and*

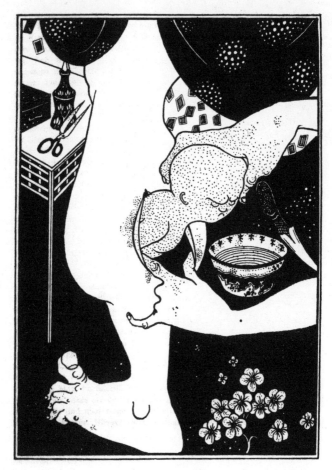

The story came out of me like a perfect birth, covered in dirt and slime.
—*Diary*, February 2, 1913

Other Stories and *Revelations of a Chambermaid* secondhand (*The Amethyst/Opals* ran ads from Viennese booksellers specializing in such rarities). He knew Mirbeau's *Torture Garden* and Sacher-Masoch's cult-making *Venus in Furs* at first hand.[3]

Kafka also certainly had in his possession (presumably, he'd borrowed Brod's review copy) another of Franz Blei's luxury subscribers-only productions—an edition of Lucian's *Conversations of the Courtesans*. Like *The Amethyst/Opals*, this would have been impossible to sell openly, for the real attraction was not the notorious classical text but the fifteen pictures by Gustav Klimt in his most definitely-not-for-public-display manner, showing *girl-on-girl legs-open action.**

Kafka spent an interesting evening in November 1911 (censored by Brod in his edition of the *Diaries*) with a distinguished collector of pilgrims' medallions and suchlike from Linz. This Herr Court Adviser had come to Prague on the recommendation of Alfred Kubin—a well-known, rather notorious writer and illustrator, a contributor to *The Amethyst/Opals,* who'd enjoyed his tour of Prague's nightlife with Kafka and Brod a couple of months before (and had recommended a certain laxative to Kafka, their having discussed each other's constipation companionably). The three men chatted about their mutual friend, the good Dr. Blei. The night culminated in a showing of the Herr Court Adviser's more private collection—of pornographic photographs, which Kafka described in considerable detail. As did he the discussions of what kind of girls their visitor best liked to have sex with (pregnant ones, as it happens) and of how a large penis, skillfully used, could so exhaust women as to reduce them to mere soulless animals.

Kafka's experiences with pornography are no chance aberration. They are part and parcel of his sexual life in these years. Because the fact is that in his early and midtwenties, Kafka's attitude toward such things was worldly, blithely cynical, sometimes even a little spooky.

On May 27, 1906, "whores" are just part of a long and jolly list of reasons (including the move of the family business) that he gave for not having seen Brod in a while. On March 29, 1908, he merrily proposed to Brod that they could have a cut-price nightlife if they went out at five or five thirty A.M., hitting the Trocadero or the Eldorado when everyone else was broke, having their girls "as

---

*Sorry, *women, alone and in pairs, in their most intimate moments,* as a current Abebooks ad for the edition (now worth thousands of dollars) more tactfully puts it.

an early breakfast." On their joint holidays, he and Brod regarded visits to brothels as an integral part of their itinerary.[4] More darkly, Kafka wrote on August 19, 1908, that he had been feeling so lonely he went with a whore "too old to still be melancholy, although she was hurt, if not surprised, that one is not so nice [*lieb*] to a whore as to a girl in an affair. Since she didn't console me, I didn't console her."

The tone here is so arctic that when you force yourself to look beyond the saccharine platitudes of the K.-myth, you simply can't help wondering unwillingly exactly *what* the immortal, hypersensitive (and by now published) Franz Kafka did, at twenty-five years of age, to have left a hardened prostitute feeling "hurt" that he hadn't been "nice" enough to her.

Intermezzo: Writing and Life

Now, none of this should shock us for the simple reason that none of it matters. No one would give a damn what Dr. Franz Kafka of Prague looked at or read or did with girls or thought or felt (let alone, what kind of hairbrush he used) if his writing had not made us stop dead and wonder, and nothing we ever find out about his life will change one iota of his work. As the Chaplain in the cathedral scene of *The Trial* says: *The text alone is unchangeable.*

The logic is inescapable: if we *needed* to know anything at all about Kafka's life to enjoy his work, no one would ever have bothered finding it out.

But this, though logically flawless, is inhuman. Being human, we want to find out *who* made things we admire. We want quite literally to *put a face* on them. And so we have with Kafka, in spades. However, the Case of Kafka's Porn shows that our picture of Kafka—the face we put to his works—is wildly skewed. And the porn is simply the most spectacular evidence of that.

Consider: We've just seen Dr. Franz Kafka in 1915, at the age of thirty-two, hypochondriac, yes, but with no medical sign whatever of actual health problems, an author already known to everyone in the know, the special protégé of Max Brod (acknowledged head of the "Prague Circle" of writers that is known throughout German-speaking culture), a man with a highly desirable day job and many useful literary friends. A writer who is being pushed (even in the middle of a world war) by a fashionable and wealthy German publishing house and has just been awarded a rather pleasant sum of money together with the very public respect of the most famous playwright of his day.

Half-winning the Fontane Prize (however it came to pass) means that he is now a paid-up insider of the most lively and respected literary culture on earth—and at a time when books still, more or less, *are* culture.*

Meanwhile, this legendary seer of Europe's fate divines the state of coming things so clearly that he invests his nest egg, of his own free will, in bonds whose value depends totally on the survival of the Austro-Hungarian Empire—and which, as things turn out, will, of course, be utterly worthless in just over three years' time.†

The question is very simple and it's this: How, for the love of God, has this real, all-too-human man become the otherworldly icon of the K.-myth, the lonely seer of Prague?

So let's now look at the most blatant example of the myth factory at work.

---

*In 1914, more people outside Germany were learning German than ever before or since—whereas Kafka's upmarket school did not even offer English as an optional subject. And whatever the language, people then simply *read far more words* than today. The newspapers of Kafka's time are so crammed as to be almost illegible to the modern eye. The streets of cities were awash with *lettering* rather than (as in mediaeval times and now) with *images*. To be a respected book-author in 1915 put you at the very top of a word-heavy cultural tree.

†Kafka's cousin Bruno made several impassioned speeches (in German) in the new Czecho-Slovak parliament, trying to get redress for ex-Bohemian holders of Austrian war-bonds (the Czechs had indeed promised to assume 33.3% of the Austrian war-debt when trying to impress President Wilson). He got nowhere before rampant inflation made the issue meaningless.

MYTH-MAKING AT WORK

An advertisement for the sanatorium where Kafka stayed in 1915,
which he chose for a little-known project the following year.

The Jackdaw and the Falcon

Our visual image of Kafka (which, because we are human, leaches inevitably into our feelings about his writings) is, as we've seen, overwhelmingly made up of that last photo of him. Well, there's another one.

This is also relatively well known. Even so, most people seeing it for the first time (which included me until I was three-quarters through my first degree) are immediately struck by the contrast between *Smiling Kafka in a Bowler Hat* and *Almost Dying Kafka* (which is quite probably the only image of Kafka they have previously seen). Quite often, amazed students paste this picture on Web sites and give it amusing titles, like *"Cool Kafka Smiles!!!"* I remember that I, too, at twenty-one, was amazed by it. I was also struck by the Charlie Chaplin hat. I only realized years later that Kafka's love of silent (that is, purely *visual*) film was probably a vital influence on his writing technique.

Not that Kafka wore that hat because he liked Charlie Chaplin, of course. Kafka wore his bowler like that because wearing a natty, side-raked bowler was the fashion among well-dressed young middle-class men of his time (which is why it was funny on Chaplin's penniless tramp).

However, once we get used to the picture, we can start to see the Kafka we know in it, after all.

Ah, yes. Of course. Those deep, veiled eyes. That wary, quizzical smile. The self-conscious irony of the pose. Yes, yes, it is our Kafka after all: all is well.

Except it isn't all well. It's not well at all. This picture is a fabrication and we are, in fact, going in completely the wrong direction if we use it to zoom in closer on Kafka.

It's no wonder we do this, for so many people have acted for so long as if the way to find out who Kafka really was and how he lived and why he wrote what he wrote and why it is so wonderful to try to get ever closer to him as a man, until at last (at some impossible point) we virtually travel through those big dark eyes and into his mysterious, private headspace, where we will find the truth about his writing.

In fact, we should be doing the opposite. We should—in this case, quite literally—be standing back a bit, seeing the wider picture, finding out a little bit more about exactly what was really going on back then and there, before any "interpretation" (or falsification) has taken place.

On the following page is the actual picture of Dr. Jackdaw and Miss Falcon—that's what their names mean in Czech—taken in or about 1908. This is the real, simple, historical artifact.

You might recognize the off-duty girl from page 33. And indeed, since we know—or at least, *can* know, if we choose—almost everything about Kafka's life, we somewhat spookily know who this long-dead waitress actually was. She was called Hansi Szokoll and sometimes described herself as an "artiste" or "modiste," making her the exact Edwardian equivalent of the sort of girl prosperous young American men-about-town today would be delighted to bed but would snidely call, behind her back, an AMW—actress/model/whatever.

No one's sure when Kafka started seeing her, but in 1908 he wrote to Max Brod about visiting her and enjoying seeing her "boyish body." According to Brod, Kafka merrily noted that "entire squadrons of cavaliers" had enjoyed that body, too. In 1912, he was still stirred to memories of Hansi while admiring a pretty chorus girl in a cabaret. The relationship seems to have gone on for at least several months.*

There was nothing at all uncommon about a prosperous young

---

*Not even distinguished native-speaking Germans have been able to explain to my (or their) satisfaction what Kafka meant when he wrote that he sat and "watched while Hansi hit her boyish body under the red sheet" (?) ("habe zugeschaut, wie sie unter der roten Decke ihren Bubenkörper schlug"). It sounds as though he had fun, though. Any suggestions?

Miss Falcon and Dr. Jackdaw, ca. 1908.

man in Prague (or Vienna, or Berlin, or Paris) having a relationship like this. Which is precisely the point. Kafka in his
midtwenties behaved simply in the way men like him behaved.

His world was one with a vast gap between rich and poor, not
just in money (our own income differentials have returned to Edwardian levels) but in what people *expected* out of life (our modern
poor have bull-headedly not yet relearned to accept their destiny
as simple fate). Prague was very well supplied with what their Viennese contemporaries famously called "sweet maidens" (they
would now be called "party girls").

These were poor working-class girls who, correctly foreseeing
that their future lives were going to contain very little in the way
of pleasure, fun, or gifts, would, while young and pretty and single, go with a well-off young man in return for being made to feel
special. And "going" with a man could sometimes mean going no
farther than to the tactfully named *chambres séparées* with which

many perfectly respectable premises were equipped—little private snugs, theoretically for intimate dinners, where you could in fact tip the waiter, lock yourselves in, and have sex right then and there—exactly as in Schnitzler's contemporary play *La Ronde* (*Reigen*).

And Prague was special in one important way. In Toulouse-Lautrec's Paris, Edward VII's London, and Klimt's Vienna, there were plenty of local "sweet girls"—but Prague had virtually no German working class to speak of. By 1910, only just over 7 percent of the population were Germans.* They functioned as a ruling caste, their dominance of industry and finance underpinned practically by preference when it came to jobs in the octopoid Habsburg bureaucracy and psychologically by German being the official language of the empire (as well as, of course, of the even more powerful empire next door). This meant that, in Prague, the sweet girls and their well-off beaux, when not speaking the international sign language of sex and money, quite literally *spoke different languages*: the girls almost invariably Czech, the men almost invariably German.

It was thus the norm for a young Prague German man of prosperous family to get his first sexual experiences from poor Slavic girls who only half-spoke his own language and were socially invisible. This is the reality behind the cutely baby-German-talking, sexually available heroine in Brod's "A Czech Serving Girl" (as seen in *The Amethyst*). It's very hard to think of any modern parallel to this situation. The nearest would probably be American clients of Latino girls in the southwest United States.

The scenario was the same wherever well-off and powerful German-speaking men (officers, civil servants, landowners, merchants) gathered in any of the dozens of demographically non-

*The term here means *German-speakers*, which is, as we'll see later, vital to recall.

German garrison towns of the Habsburg Empire. Prague, however, was unique in providing a modern, metropolitan, electric-lit setting for this theater of Germanic sexual imperialism.*

What such erotic apartheid did to the heads of the young men concerned isn't hard to imagine. Kafka's powerful sexual imagination seems to have been forever haunted by poor young servant-girl figures. In *Amerika*,[1] Karl is exiled because of an affair with a maid; in *The Trial*, Josef K's sexual odyssey comprises a typist (the modern male executive's servant girl), a washerwoman, and the lawyer's maid; in *The Castle*, Frieda is a barmaid and Pepi (at first) an even lower class of servant. In *The Metamorphosis*, the young pigtailed maid is particularly terrified of Gregor (whereas the old one is not afraid at all).

Like the courtesans of the classical world (on whose habits Kafka, as we saw, read up with help from Klimt's graphic illustrations), girls like Hansi Szokoll weren't public whores. They weren't available to just anyone and they didn't take cash. But if you knew the rules of the social dance, and played your cards and your presents right, they were there and waiting—in places like the Café Corso, one of Kafka's and Brod's favorite haunts a century ago, which was (as the *Prague Daily News* put it waspishly on March 31, 1907) "where the Beautiful Things of the ballet, of the cabarets and of Prague capitalism get together to balance the books after business hours."

Around the time this photo was taken, Brod's diary also noted Kafka's retiring to a *chambre séparée* at the Trocadero with a girl whose rent he offered to pay and who "looked like the picture of Germania on German postage stamps"—that is, large, blond, and rather terrifying.

---

*We don't need imagination to re-create *this* aspect of Kafka's Prague. The city that sells itself with his face is again a mecca for Western men eager for Slavic girls, who, being still poor and available, are still alleged to be wildly erotic. Thanks to two World Wars and one Cold War, however, the girls speak broken English rather than broken German—and the clients are gone next day, not living round the corner and pretending nothing ever happened.

The Curious Case of the Dog in the Picture

So here they are, a young lawyer and his actress/model/whatever (or rather, *one* of them) back in about 1908. By applying normal human psychology to this pair (and remember: why on earth should we apply any *other* kind of psychology?), we can make various entertaining guesses about how it came to pass that these two young people sat in a studio for this photograph, and what they were thinking as their moment together was immortalized.

Did hard-working Hansi the waitress-cum-artiste get her rich, handsome boyfriend to sit down with her and have their photo taken as a sign that he *did* really like her, and not just *like that?* Did lucky Franz get her to sit and be photographed with him so he could show this girl off to his bachelor friends? Were they just having such a good time one day that they decided on the spur of the moment to go into a studio and have their photo taken? Is Kafka's quizzical smile and self-conscious pose due to his wondering whether having one's picture formally and semipublically taken in a studio with one's waitress-sweetheart was such a great idea after all? Or do we think, like Alt, that they look as though they have "climbed straight out of a *chambre séparée*"?

And what about the dog in the photograph?

This isn't a joke question. Remember: this is a posed studio photograph, not a casual snapshot. Nothing that's here is here by mere chance. Who put the dog there, and why? Is this photograph all a stage-managed erotic mis-en-scène for the intellectual titillation of Max Brod and other fellow insiders, bold readers perhaps, like Kafka at this time of his life, of *The Amethyst* and *Opals?*

Erotic? Well, Kafka was certainly acquainted with Baron Sacher-Masoch's infamous *Venus in Furs.* And, being far taller than the average man of his day, he must have towered above Hansi Szokoll in real life. Yet in this pose he appears to be no taller than her, if indeed as tall. Is he literally *making himself small* (like the narrators of so many of his tales), while Hansi sits tall and smiles broadly, showing her teeth?* Is this photograph all a setup, an in-joke reference to Kafka's undoubted masochism?[2]

Now, this may seem like some overheated suggestion of a Kafka code, but remember how many undoubted facts about Kafka have already seemed surprising.

Remember that the hero of Sacher-Masoch's story allows himself to be treated "like a dog." In the original German, this reads *"wie ein Hund"*—which are the very same words, his *last* words, uttered by Josef K. in the final sentence of *The Trial*. Remember, too, the name of the hero of *The Metamorphosis*. Gregor Samsa. A very unusual name—or is it not so much a name as a key: SAcher-MASoch, perhaps? After all, when the hero of *Venus in Furs* is renamed by his pitiless mistress as part of his degradation, what is his name changed to? *Gregor.*

Coincidence really seems an insufficient explanation here. Sir Malcolm Pasley, who knew Kafka's writings backward and forward (he showed me the originals in his own study) often referred to what he called "Kafka's semiprivate games"; this may well be one of them.

Well, we shall never know what Kafka is thinking about as he sits next to Hansi and strokes the dog, and why he had the photograph taken, but it seems a safe bet that he is *not* thinking about the dark looming clouds of human history, the hopelessness of life, or the "terrible conflicts of his day-to-day existence" (Hayman).

Hansi, Airbrushed

You would perhaps have thought that having been the named and photographically identifiable sweetheart, or at any rate the regular sexual playmate, of the most recognizable author of the twentieth century would have earned a girl at least a little corner in literary history.

---

*Kafka—notably in *The Metamorphosis*, *A Country Doctor* and *A Hunger-Artist*—uses images of teeth to indicate mercilessly (in Nietzsche's sense "healthily") self-serving Life.

Not a bit of it. She's not even named in some biographies and, even where she is, she never gets more than a single paragraph. Sweet Hansi Szokoll has been cropped from history: the Kafka industry has airbrushed away her little piece of immortality.

A girl with whom Kafka certainly never had sex—"the Swiss girl" he fell for briefly while on holiday in Riva (and while engaged to Felice) and whom he only ever referred to by her initials of G.W.—is mentioned copiously in every book. People are so eager to provide her with an identity that even forgeries have been used to do it.[3] But no one has researched Hansi Szokoll. Every other utterance Kafka ever made, or is alleged to have made, on the topic of sex is pored over by troops of scholars. Yet Hansi, who certainly had sex of some kind or another with Kafka, apparently over an extended period, and who is surely the closest model we know for his many lower-class erotic female figures, is to all intents and purposes utterly ignored.

Well, the notion of Franz Kafka's being a well-groomed young professional man-about-town with money aplenty in his pockets (he lived at home and didn't pay rent, after all), who enthusiastically frequented brothels and regularly consorted with a penniless but pretty waitress/artiste of whom he had fond memories years later, hardly agrees with the icon of the tortured quasi-saintly genius—any more than do the facts that Kafka liked porn, laughed aloud as he read his work, or invested heavily in the Austro-German war effort.

And when the facts we have before us sit uncomfortably with the myth we *want*, it's the myth that wins out, every time.

Kafka and Hitler, or The Perils of Hindsight

There are myths and there are myths. The trouble with our myth of Kafka is that it's dictated by hindsight—that cheapest, unbranded form of wisdom that simply gets handed out to one and all, as the years go by. Ah, if only we had bought *that* house *then* at *that* price! Little did we know . . .

Hindsight allows us to make all sorts of wonderfully entertaining but absolutely meaningless connections. We'll now see how.

From Eduardova to Josefine

Kafka's world-famous diary was kick-started not by some literary event, or by a family feud, or by some dark thought about the hopelessness of life, but—it will, I hope, by now come as no surprise to learn—by an erotically charged night at the theater (that paradise, then as now, for the sophisticated voyeur).

The first five entries in the diary are simple images, none of them even thirty words long—but the sixth, seventh, eighth, and ninth paragraphs (that is, the first substantial ones) are a series of miniatures about a dancer called Yevgenya Eduardova who, as he wrote years later, haunted Kafka's dreams for months with her wild czardas.

The first two of these Eduardova fragments are remembered dreams that Kafka noted down (all through his life, Kafka, befitting a man who at least knew of Freud's basic ideas, set a great store by his dreams as a source of insight and inspiration). The third piece is a charming miniature that, like so much Romantic literature, is about a life dedicated to Art and the effect of that Art on Ordinary Folk, here represented by the rather uptight narrator. Kafka describes the dreamlike scene as if it were simply reported reality, showing an early, sunlit example of his central technique.

The dancer Eduardova, a great lover of music, always travels with two violinists at her side, often commanding them to play, and she does it on the tram just the same as anywhere else. There's no law against playing on the tram, after all, so long as the music's good,

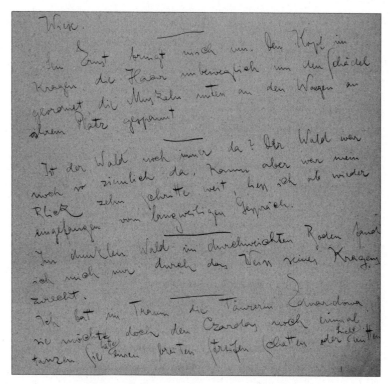

The start of something big. Eduordova is mentioned in the
third line from the bottom, and her czardaz the line after.

the other passengers like it and it's free, i.e., no one passes the hat
around afterward. It *is* rather surprising at first and for a while everyone says they find it inappropriate. But when you're really rattling
along, with wind in your hair in a quiet street, it does sound nice.

The last Eduardova fragment reads like the start of something
much bigger: it's a scene-setting piece that muses cooly, almost
clinically, on the nature of the dancer's attractiveness—or rather,
on the conundrum of the fact that she's actually nothing special,
looks rather like an aunt, is almost ugly, so much so that she's

often treated as nothing special at all even by people who know she's a famous dancer.*

Eduardova makes a fascinating curtain-raiser, a first glimpse into how Kafka came to write the sort of things he wrote. First comes the initial dreamlike or literally dreamed-up image, an electric charge of eroticism straight from the subconscious, which is then transformed and harnessed by the act of writing it down, spinning it out, playing with it.

Nietzsche said that we are all barrel organs with only one tune but with eternity itself turning the handle, and this applies to Kafka maybe more than to any other great writer. The fourth piece about Eduardova, that ninth diary entry, is hauntingly like a pre-echo of Kafka's final story, "Josefine the Singer": there, just as here, a female stage-artiste, a barnstorming diva, is discussed by a detached, observant male narrator who tries to unpick the mystery of how a woman can be so ordinary in life and so worshipped on the stage.

The arc from the young would-be writer starting his diary in 1909 with thoughts of Eduardova the dancer to the dying writer of 1924 correcting the proofs of "Josefine the Singer" vaults the entirety of Kafka's writings. Like Goethe's Faust, he is incessantly drawn on by the theatrical magic of *eternal femininity*. It is surely no coincidence that his final love, Dora Dymant, the woman with whom he seems at last to have found happiness, was an actress.

Well, this is the dancer who sparked off Kafka's first major diary entries.

Kafka saw her on the Petersburg Ballet's tour in Prague on May 24 or 25, 1909 (see how much we know about his life, poor man!). It was not only his dreams she haunted, no doubt. Ballet stars were goddesses in the Edwardian world and Eduardova (who

---

*This illustrates something profound about Kafka. Whenever he's strongly drawn to a woman, for whatever reason, he immediately starts to list her physical flaws. His first account to Max Brod of Hedwig Weiler, whom he went on to write to for years, does this, as does his first diary entry about Felice. It's as if he's trying to control his own darkly yearning psyche by *making* himself see things superficially—which is, interestingly, just what Wilde and Nietzsche said the Greeks did.

Eduardova the Dancer.

is now forgotten) was internationally famous as the more sensual counterpoint to Pavlova (who still at least has a dessert named after her). A man in 1909 who sat in the theater and stared open mouthed at Yevgenya Eduardova's flashing thighs, Slavic passion, and whirling skirts was about as unusual and individual as a man in 2008 unable to take his eyes off Beyoncé's booty on MTV.

But little did Kafka know that the figure who thus inspired the most famous literary diary of the twentieth century was to have a curious erotic connection with the author of the only German book of the twentieth century that is more internationally famous than Kafka's works.

Some years after Kafka lost sleep over memories of her uninhibited moves, Eduardova became the decisive teacher of another soon-to-be famous and sexually devastating dancer. This dancer became the first-ever girl to get a solo spot at Max Rheinhardt's famous cabaret, and, like her teacher Eduardova, but in a new, supercharged, postwar way, she drove men wild with her suggestions of scarily irresistible female sexuality. Eduardova's pupil captivated this other German author, who was born only six years after Kafka and only a couple of hours' steam-train journey from Prague, a citizen of the same Habsburg Empire as Kafka himself.

Leni Riefenstahl (for she it was) enraptured Adolf Hitler (for he, of course, it is), becoming the Third Reich's very own Aryan goddess, her notorious film *Triumph of the Will* mythologizing that little, grotesquely Chaplin-esque man whom fate chose as the nemesis of Kafka's (and for that matter his own) whole culture.

So: Kafka was entranced by Eduardova who taught Riefenstahl who entraced Adolf Hitler. What an uncanny connection!

Except it is nothing of the sort. The line connecting Kafka, Eduardova, Riefenstahl, and Hitler is real, yes, and perhaps it is the kind of thing that may have some place in some freewheeling psycho-history of male images of women in the early twentieth century, but as far as understanding Kafka's writing goes, it is as dependent on hindsight, and hence as utterly meaningless, as is pointing out (as all books on Kafka never tire of doing) that Kafka's entire extended family *would become* victims of the Holocaust.

Which sounds shocking. But let me explain.

Kafka and the Holocaust

The Holocaust is the surest proof that there is, in our world, absolute evil that we ignore at our peril and with which there can be no negotiation. Anyone who dares to cheapen it by using that word about any other event (in hideous phrases like "a cultural holocaust" or "an ecological holocaust") is a fool or worse. There is only one thing called the Holocaust. The Holocaust creates such darkness visible that, silhouetted against it, even the Red Army appears briefly as force of light.[4]

But the Holocaust is utterly meaningless when considering the writings of Dr. Franz Kafka (1883–1924) of Prague.

In fact, it is worse than meaningless. It destroys meaning, sucks meaning into that blackest of holes. The Holocaust is the shadow we *have* to make ourselves forget in the context of Kafka. Because it's the darkest event in our history, it's the hardest to ignore: but we simply *have* to, however hard that may be, if we're ever going to be able to see anything in Kafka but the myth.

So when a recent biographer of Kafka (Nicholas Murray) writes with a straight face of "the long-standing debate about whether Kafka foresaw the fate of the Jews in Nazi Europe," I throw his book across the room. *Foresaw?* Sorry, what is he trying to say? That history is prewritten? That it is all out there already, just sitting and waiting? This is no *debate*, this is plain and simple tripe that belongs in *Star Trek* or *Dr. Who*.

The Nazification of Germany wasn't some historically inevitable process (though that was how the Nazis themselves always presented it). There was nothing *to* "foresee" even in 1928, never mind in 1915. Even after the Nuremberg Laws, even after Kristallnacht, even after the outbreak of war and *even* after the foul, on-the-spot massacres in Russia and the Baltic states, the Shoah, the systematic and planned extermination of European Jewry, was not a done deal until the notorious (and stenographically preserved) Wannsee Conference. Only after Wannsee did the whole state apparatus of Nazi Germany put itself at the service of fulfilling Hitler's psychotic anti-Semitism. Only then did it attain that escape velocity that propelled it beyond even the likes of Stalin, into hitherto uncharted spheres of human evil. But Wannsee would and could never have happened without a unique and *completely unpredictable* concatenation of elements.

The first among these were the votes of millions of Germans (largely delivered by the miscalculation of the law-abiding Nationalist boss, Hugenberg, who controlled vast swaths of the press and the newsreels), the machinations of von Papen, the moral bankruptcy of the German army, and the suicidal insanity of the Communists.* Then came the craven refusal of Britain, France, and America to see what was in front of their noses. But the most important and direct cause of the Shoah was the fact that Hitler successfully deceived his ally, Stalin. This, aided by the incompetent tactics of the recently purged Red Army in the opening months of the battle, allowed vast tracts of land and millions of Jews to fall briefly but fatally into Hitler's hands on a front where murder was (quite literally) the order of the day. After that, there was simply no way to stop the Holocaust without first smashing the Wehrmacht—the majority of whose leaders had long thought of Slavs as quasi-colonial subjects, hated Communists almost as murderously as Hitler did, and simply didn't give a damn about the Jews one way or another.

To suggest that all this was somehow "foreseeable" to a writer in Prague before, during, and just after the First World War is not only philosophical balderdash, it is crassly insulting to the memory of the millions on the spot who did not "foresee" it even when it came knocking on their doors—and so stepped without resistance onto trains bound for nowhere still believing, like Elie Wiesel's father, that the nation of Goethe and Beethoven, however perverted, must have *some* rational plan for them.[5]

No: however hard it is, we *have* to try to look back without see-

---

*Many people would add, the pusillanimity of the Catholic Center Party. But the fact is that between 1928 and 1932 Nazi electoral success was driven by breakthroughs in *Protestant* regions. It's rather tough to blame Catholic politicians for not stopping a rot they didn't start.

ing things through the dark mirror of the Holocaust. We will not get far with Kafka until we are able to put that unforeseeable future out of mind and see the reality of his own day.

We can see this very clearly if we travel to a place that, very bizarrely, figures hardly if at all in most biographies.

Bizarrely, for two reasons: first, because it's to do with the part of his life that would actually most deserve canonization (it led to an official request from wounded servicemen themselves that Dr. Kafka should be awarded a medal); and second, because it's hard to see how people have been able to resist writing historical fiction or making clever films about Franz Kafka's many visits to war-damaged mental patients, at a sanatorium he greatly helped to found, in a place called Frankenstein. . . .

Folk Comrade Dr. Kafka of Frankenstein

Kafka's involvement with mentally damaged servicemen has hardly been studied at all, even though the place where it occurred still exists and sits there waiting as a ready-made film set.

Perhaps Dr. Kafka's work in Frankenstein makes people uncomfortable because it reveals one thing that we so easily forget—and perhaps *want* to forget—about Kafka. It shows that right up to the fall of the Habsburg Empire, *Kafka identified completely with the German-speaking community* of what was to become Czechoslovakia.

This is stunningly clear when we read the public proclamation that Kafka personally drew up in November 1916 to kick-start the sanatorium. Signed (along with a hundred other Prague luminaries) by himself and his bosses Dr. Pribram and Dr. Marschner, it is a fascinating document in many ways, but the most striking thing is the first word, the word Kafka uses as the headline of his appeal:

VOLKSGENOSSEN!

As anyone who has ever read anything about the Third Reich will know, this term, "folk-comrades," was the everyday word in Hitler's Germany to mean "good fellow Germans" (as opposed to "folk betrayers" and "subhumans").

And it's not some aberration because, throughout this document, with its moving depiction of the shattered nerves of returning soldiers, Kafka uses language that a mere ten years later could only be used by ultra-nationalist, anti-Semitic German right-wingers.

> On October 14, in the German House in Prague, a meeting took place of representatives from all the parties, classes, and regions of German Bohemia. With rare unanimity and readiness to contribute, the need for effective help was recognized and it was decided to found a German Society for the Building and Maintenance of a Soldiers' and People's Mental Health Institute in German Bohemia based in Prague. This society is intended to be part of the German-Bohemian popular effort in the care of war victims and will for the time being be represented by the committee which was elected at the above meeting. The first task is to create the financial means. To this end we appeal to you to take part in this great German-Bohemian mission, the like of which nothing exists in Austria . . .

This institute would be "reserved for the war-damaged of German-Bohemia" for the duration of the war and for as long as need be afterward, but would then become a permanent recourse for general "mentally ill German-Bohemian folk-comrades."

There is no mention in Kafka's press release of any sense of solidarity or fellow feeling with war-damaged Czech (or any other) soldiers of Franz Josef's multinational army, let alone any intention to actually help them. Kafka is appealing to German-speaking folk comrades on behalf of German-speaking folk comrades, period.

Now, it would be very easy to say that in this appeal Kafka was asking for money from a certain gang of people and therefore trimming his language to *their* tastes. But this won't do. We have Kafka's private letters and diaries to compare. These show that in cultural and political matters, he simply used the current terminology of German-speakers in Prague without a second thought.

For example, in his appeal, when he said "Austria," what did he mean? Not the country we now know as Austria—but what was *then* meant by "Austria," that is, the whole western half of the Habsburg Empire.* He used the same word in exactly the same way in his private diary when he wrote about his "sadness at the Austrian defeats" or the difficulty he would have finding legal work "outside Austria."

In one of his early letters to Felice he noted that the result of the Second Balkan War (which left Serbia as a mini-superpower in the Balkans) was "a great blow to our colonies." Now, the Habsburg Empire *had* no colonies in the French or British sense. What Kafka meant here is Austria's 1908 annexations in the Balkans—her "colonies" in Europe itself (the military occupation of which had very nearly led to war with Russia). As Stach says, "The ease with which Kafka parroted the official jargon is disconcerting."†

Disconcerting, that is, to anyone who clings to the K.-myth. This is a fine example of where that myth clearly blocks the truth. No one *wants* to know this about Franz Kafka. People interested in the culture of Prague don't want to be reminded that Kafka was a paid-up and active member, right until the end, of the German-speaking

---

*"Cisleithania" is the wonderfully fictional-sounding name historians use.

†Especially when you consider the argument that Nazi vileness on the Eastern Front was rooted in a tradition of Germany seeing its Slav neighbors rather as other powers saw non-Europeans—i.e. as people simply *worth* less.

élite. Literary theorists don't want Kafka to use terms of "political discourse" so uncritically. Readers keen on Kafka's Jewishness don't want him to be so deeply German. And many Germans find it easier not to be reminded that a place called *German Bohemia* ever existed, never mind that its self-proclaimed citizens include the greatest modern German writer.

A couple of months after his appeal to his folk comrades, on December 9, 1916, Kafka wrote to Felice bemoaning the fact that he heard too late about some "valuable lectures" given in Berlin, among them one by the poet (and fellow German Jew) Rudolf Borchardt, called "The War and the German Decision." The lecture is nowhere preserved, but given that Borchardt worked for the press office of the general staff, pleaded for the renewal of German culture by a spiritual-leader figure and was later an admirer of Mussolini (before being hounded to death by the Nazis), it is unlikely that what Kafka called his "valuable" public wartime lecture was either pacifist or culturally inclusive in tone.

Kafka Dreams of Dark-Uniformed Prussian Guardsmen

There's simply no way around this one. However hard we find it to take—and remember, we only find it hard to take *because* of the K.-myth—the truth is that although he spoke fluent Czech and took, for a German-speaker, an unusual interest in the Czech culture of 90 percent of his fellow Pragers (he often went, for example, to the Czech National Theater), Kafka's basic identification was totally with German-speaking culture.

If, for example, our only evidence for Prague street names in Kafka's day was Kafka's diaries and letters, we would have absolutely no inkling that throughout his writing life, those Prague streets were actually signposted—then as now—*only* in Czech (as a result of sustained and sometimes violent pressure from Czech nationalists). Yet Kafka *always* used the German versions without thinking, even when writing to his Czech lover, Milena.

The German-speaking hegemony in Middle Europe collapsed in late 1918 as quickly and shockingly as communism did in late 1989. But right up to the end, Kafka no more foresaw this than anyone else did.*

We, who have the dubious benefit of hindsight, might think that, by the end of 1917, it was obvious that Germany and Austria-Hungary were not going to win the war. It's easy for us to see that America (in at last) was striding out from the wings of world history, its famous Big Stick now firmly in hand. But it seemed far more important to Germans and Austrians *at the time* that Russia, the most deeply feared enemy, had been knocked right out and forced to cede vast territories.†

As late as March 1918, Bruno Kafka, in his capacity as one of the leaders of the German-Bohemian Folk-Comrades, made an official complaint to Vienna that (Max Brod's) translation of Janáček's opera *Jenůfa*, being originally a *Czech* work, should not have been performed in the Viennese Imperial Opera.‡

In Cousin Franz's case, this identification with (and trust in) the German hegemony was so deep that it ruled even his now-famous unconscious. On November 10, 1917, Kafka dreamed that he was an Austrian solder in the Battle of Tagliamento (a notable Austro-German victory, much-reported in October and November), which was going very badly for him and his comrades:

> Great despair, general flight is going to be necessary. Then a Prussian major appears—he's in fact been with us the whole time, watching the battle, but the way he now steps forward into the suddenly

---

*Any more than any of the scores of university experts on East Germany foresaw in the summer of 1989 that they would soon have nothing to be experts *about*.

†In 1941, an Austro-German warlord, his eye firmly on Russia, would again fatally underestimate British resilience and U.S. reach.

‡It was after having gone to Berlin to attend a production of this opera that Brod accompanied Kafka on his final retreat to his parents' apartment in 1924.

empty space makes him appear as though for the first time. He sticks two fingers of each hand in his mouth and whistles, the way you whistle for a dog, but lovingly. This is the sign for a troop of men who have been waiting nearby and who now march forward. They are Prussian Guards, young, quiet men, not many, maybe only a company of them, and they all seem to be officers: at least, they all carry long sabers and their uniforms are dark. As they now march past us with short steps, slowly pushing forward, now and then looking at us, the way they completely accept the inevitability of their walk into death is at once moving, uplifting and a token of victory. The intervention of these men is my deliverance, and I awake.

Which leaves little room for doubt as to where Kafka's deepest feelings (as well as his pension fund) were invested.*

Kafka's political mind-set was still unconsciously prewar even after the decision had gone against Germanic rule in Mitteleuropa. When he found in 1920 that visiting Milena was complicated because, to get from Prague to a train station in Austria, you now needed a passport (well, you *would*, they now being separate countries), Kafka—who by this time was an even more senior official in the pay of the new Czech state—threw up his hands in despair at this "idiotic business of passports."

It is naturally very hard for us, now, to see how on earth, being Jewish, Kafka could think so highly (and so deeply) of the Germans. But the way things *are* is not the way things *had to be*, and this question brings us to the greatest test of our historical imagination.

---

*Kafka's dream perfectly mirrors the mind-set of Prague's German-speakers, who, as 1917 wore into 1918, began increasingly to fear that "the Monarchy" might sacrifice them to the Czechs as part of a federal settlement—and to look to "the Reich" for backup. This makes a very important point: that Kafka's subconscious plumbs his time and place so revealingly because he *belongs so thoroughly to it*.

Jews, Germans, and Anti-Semites

There is actually nothing bizarre or uncanny at all about the fact that, as a Jew, Kafka in 1916 repeatedly used the word *Volksgenossen* (folk comrades) in a public document. Or that he should identify wholeheartedly with the German-speakers of Bohemia. Or that he should long, even in his dreams, for a German-Austrian victory in the Great War.

Yes, within a very few years, the term *folk comrade* would become the unmistakable property of the extreme (and anti-Semitic) right. Yes, the strong feeling of the German-speakers of Bohemia that they belonged to Austria or perhaps even to Germany, not to Czechoslovakia, would become one of Hitler's strongest cards in hamstringing the democratic response to his aggression. Yes, within twenty years it would become impossible for a Jew (or, for that matter, any friend of civilization) to see dark-uniformed German soldiers as anything but mortal enemies.

But the damning words here, as with the Holocaust, are: *would become.* This combination should be banned in principle from any book about Kafka, for it is the giveaway sign of a biographer who has failed to escape the fatal gravity of hindsight.

The word *Volksgenossen*, for example, was not originally a Nazi term at all: it was stolen from the non-Marxist wing of the Socialists, who had coined it in the 1890s to stress that they didn't want Engels's class war (and his centralized party). So when Kafka uses it in his 1916 appeal—and even in his 1924 story, "Josefine the Singer"—we must beware any temptation to let our hindsight rip.

It all goes to show how firmly we have to keep history and chronology (those deadly enemies of myth) in mind. And nothing illustrates this so much as the relationship between Jews and Germans in Kafka's day.

Natural Allies

The German and Austrian empires before 1914 still demanded a very thick skin from any Jew who wanted the final social acceptance of a commission in the Imperial Reserve (like Arthur Schnitzler) or a position as a senior civil servant (like Kafka). But Jews *did* make it like this and the barriers to their doing so were little if at all worse than in, say, contemporary France. Britain had had a Jewish PM, Disraeli but, even there, and certainly in the United States, there were plenty of clubs in 1910 that Jews would simply never get to join.

The legal position of the Jews in Germany and Austria was getting more normalized with every passing decade. To be sure, there were social insults, secret and not so secret. Arthur Schnitzler talked scornfully of people who "stuff themselves at the Jews' dinner tables and start attacking them the moment they step out of the door." The notorious mayor of Vienna, Karl Lueger, was an anti-Semitic rabble-rouser. But Lueger's cynicism ("I decide who's a Jew here," he famously replied when challenged about his own Jewish friends) was simply part of the general atmosphere of ethnic tension and irresponsible stake-upping that was everywhere in the last decades of the Habsburg Empire.

Everyone could be as loud as he wanted in meetings and demonstrations because everyone knew that, in the end, Germanic *Ordnung* would be maintained. Some kind of deal would be done. The most successful and cunning rival demagogues from the various national factions—German, Czech, Hungarian, Slovenian, whatever—would, having delivered their supporters, sit down together, like Northern Ireland's Dr. Ian Paisley and Mr. Gerry Adams, to divvy up the plums from the central government they had so often sworn to overthrow.*

Kaiser Franz Josef was the ultimate safeguard. No government headed by him would ever tolerate the sheer, blatant *illegality* and

---

*Which is exactly what von Papen & Co. expected to happen with Hitler in 1933.

disorder of pogroms, never mind sponsor them (as the czars did). Again and again, Franz Josef refused to appoint Lueger mayor of Vienna even after his election victories, simply because he doubted Lueger's adherence to the rule of law. If need be (as need had indeed been in Prague in 1887), an army that was largely German-officered and gave its orders exclusively in German (the Kaiser always personally insisted on this, even at the cost of outraging his otherwise hyperloyal Hungarians) would quell anti-Jewish disturbances, the same way as they would quell any disturbances too big for the police to cope with: with fixed bayonets and loaded guns.

The Kaiser's "loyal subjects of the Mosaic confession" were not loyal out of stupidity, but because Germanic *Ordnung* was good for them. More than anyone else, Jews had reason to agree with the thoughts the great Goethe, himself, had put into the mouth of his heroic figure, Egmont: "Better a little unfreedom than a lot of disorder."

To assimilate, to *become* German, was easy and natural for Jews because the lingua franca of Eastern European Jewry, Yiddish, is (despite post-Holocaust claims by people who don't want it to be true) essentially a form of German, arguably just an extreme eastern dialect of German.* The 1913 International Zionist Congress, which Kafka visited, was held in Vienna, and German was its formal language, as it had been for all the previous congresses and would remain until the twenties.

In short, to Central European Jews before the Great War, the Germans were the natural allies. To Zionists, indeed, Berlin was a sort of provisional capital en route to the Promised Land.†

---

*The comparison is always made between Yiddish and High German, i.e. the equivalent of "BBC English." But a Yiddish-speaking street-trader from Warsaw asking directions from a working-class Dresdener in 1910 would have had less trouble making himself understood than would a Tyrolean peasant lost in Hamburg today.

†This seemed so clear to the future editor of *The Times*, Henry Wickham Steed, that on the eve of the Great War he became a raving anti-Semite *because* he was so anti-German.

Prague Mathematics

Prague was a special case. There were, in 1910, 32,000 Germans in Prague and 28,000 Jews. But this doesn't mean that there were 32,000 Germans *and* 28,000 Jews, because the figures were in answer to two different census questions, the vital one for Prague being, "What language do you normally use?"

This was the important question (as it is, for example, in Welsh-speaking areas of Wales or French-speaking areas of Canada today). This was what really mattered politically in multi-cultural, multifaith Prague: not what your grandfather was called, or whether you were Catholic, Hussite or Jew, but *what language you daily spoke.*

So the census figure that there were 32,000 "Germans" in Prague in 1910 actually means that *there were 32,000 people in Prague in 1910 who said that German was their principal language*—which includes a very large number of its 28,000 Jews.

The number is a moot point, but getting somewhere near to an answer is vital if we want to feel the reality of Kafka's life in Prague as a culturally German Jew.

In 1910, 55 percent of Prague's 28,000 Jews declared themselves to be linguistic *Czechs*. This was a big change from the 1890 census, in which 75 percent of them had checked "German." The famous story goes that being "Czech" had saved Hermann Kafka's shop from the anti-German/Jewish riots of 1897: "Kafka's all right, he's a Czech," was allegedly the cry as other German/Jewish shops were torched. This may suggest why more and more Jews declared themselves to speak Czech during the next two decades.

In 1910, this would mean that there were about 13,000 Jews who still checked "German" as their main language, leaving about 19,000 non-Jewish Germans in Prague.

But that's almost certainly untrue. People often say in censuses what they want to be true of themselves or wish to have believed about them.[6] Whatever their parents told the officials, *fully 90 percent of Jewish children* in Prague were sent (as was Kafka, son of the "Czech" Hermann) to self-consciously German-language, Goethe-teaching, patriotically Habsburg schools, right up until 1918.

Hence, even of the 15,000 allegedly "Czech" Jews in 1910, the vast majority of them would have had a German-speaking Austrian education, making German their natural language of culture and business. Which means that, in 1910, when 32,000 people checked "German" as their language, there were 19,000 non-Jewish Germans in Prague plus about 13,000 declaredly German-speaking Jews *plus* maybe as many as 13,500 Jews who (whatever they had said in the census) were culturally "Germans."

The exact figures are probably impossible to work out. Ernst Pawel concludes that as many as 85 percent of German-speakers in Prague before the war were Jews, though I don't follow his math. At any rate, it's obvious that the oft-peddled notion that Prague Jews were "a minority within a minority" is plainly wrong.

The day-to-day reality of Kafka's life was that at any German-language cultural event there would be at least as many Jewish German-Bohemians in the room as non-Jewish German-Bohemians, and probably more. Whatever may have been the case in Vienna, Prague had no "glass ceiling" for Jews; for instance, the members of the most exclusive of Prague's German-language institutions, the Casino Club, were 48 percent Jewish.

In fact, in 1910 Prague, what we now see as anti-Semitism was really anti-*Germanism*. Kafka's friend Oscar Baum was not blinded in a fight with Czech schoolboys because he was Jewish—but because he was walking to a German school.* This is a model for the

---

*His only son was killed in Israel by Jewish terrorists because he was sitting in hotel used by the British Army.

whole conflict: the Jews of Prague were attacked not because they were Jews as such, not because of *what they were*, but because of the *political/linguistic choice they had made.*

The Jews had freely chosen to throw in their lot with the Germans. It was plain to the impatient Czechs that without the cultural support—gratuitous, from their point of view—of the overwhelming majority of the Jews, the centuries-old struggle between Czechs and Germans would long since have been decided by sheer weight of Czech numbers. To Czech nationalists in Prague and to various local patriots in smaller towns across the Habsburg Empire, the Jews pretty much *were* the Germans.*

It is so hard to re-imagine through the blackness of the Holocaust, that the only way is to nail ourselves to the mast of real artifacts and stop our ears to the siren song of hindsight.

Let us turn to the new century's eve issue, December 31, 1899, of Kafka's (and his parents' and all their friends') daily paper, our old friend the *Prague Daily News.*

One of the stories is a curious one about a disturbance in the offices of the Workers' Accident Insurance Institute for the Kingdom of Bohemia, which led to the arrest of a certain disgruntled client by the name of Josef Kafka. Perhaps, when he later worked in that very office, Kafka heard this entertaining story about a Josef K. and went back to this very paper to check it out? Who knows?

But in that newspaper is something we can know about and should care about. This editorial piece shows *without hindsight* what the German/Jewish population of Prague were reading and thinking right then in Kafka's formative years.

This final editorial of the nineteenth century in Prague's most important newspaper expresses, in high-flown German and Gothic

---

*Slavic locals, used for generations to seeing the Jews as supporters of Germanic power, often saw the Holocaust as some bizarre inter-German warfare which they could watch, if not with pleasure, then certainly without feeling any need to intervene.

> Czechen seitdem hingerathen?! Schade um das begabte Volk, das verjüngt einer schönen Renaissance entgegenging! Schade, daß es seine besten Kräfte vergeudet, verleitet von selbst-süchtigen Wortführern, von einem Abel, der im Verein mit dem Clericalismus in der Zwie-tracht des freisinnigen Bürgerthums seine letzte Rettung steht; schade, daß mittelalterlicher Wahn um sich greifen konnte, die Furie des Anti-semitismus! Begehrlich gemacht durch die Er-folge bei schwächlichen Regierungen und in dem von Obstruction zu Obstruction wankenden todeskranken Parlament sehen die Führer dieses Volkes im politischen Kampf dessen ganze Zu-kunft, versprechen sie sich von diesem alle Früchte, die nur auf dem Boden friedlicher Cultur durch positive Arbeit gedeihen können.

Prager Tagblatt editorial from December 31st, 1899.

type, the hope that, in the coming new century, the "medieval lu-nacy of anti-Semitism" will be abandoned—*by the Czechs*.

This sentiment remained the case throughout Kafka's life. True, he claimed it was a miracle that he, as a Jew, had gotten his excellent job in German Bohemia, but Max Brod also had one of those longed-for six-hour day jobs. To steal Kafka's own Kierkegaar-dian way of putting things, a miracle that has come to pass, never mind twice, is by definition no miracle.

It is only after the Great War, which of course changed every-thing, that Kafka ever records actual anti-Semitic remarks from Germans (and this wasn't in Prague) or mentions, even half-jokingly, any potential physical threat from Germans (he doesn't want to go to a sanatorium in Bavaria because "there they only take Jews so they can kill them").

Even after the war, the real and present danger to Kafka as a Prague Jew came from the same direction it had done all his life.

In November 1920, he famously reused his "bug" motif in a letter to Milena, trying to describe what it felt like to have to live amid the "bath of Jew-hating" in the streets of Prague, only surviving thanks to the protection of the police. In Czech Prague in 1920, as in 1887, it was the Czechs who were the window-smashing (and this time, scroll-burning) anti-Semites. The new state's army had to be called in when even mounted police couldn't cope—whereas in German Berlin three years later, Kafka, even though the political situation was generally very tense and he very ill, could go without the slightest fear to Jewish events and institutions, or stand in the breadlines of the *Inflationswinter* "experiencing the feeling of community with an unhappy people in an unhappy time."[7]

It's heartbreaking to read this now, of course, but everything about Europe before the Holocaust is heartbreaking. Masaryk's bravery and skill in defusing Czech anti-Semitism can't let us shirk the historical facts. If we don't want to fall for the K.-myth, our motto, however unpalatable the results, must be:

HINDSIGHT VERBOTEN!*

With this firmly in mind, we'll now go on to look at some of the planks of the K.-myth, and we'll start by sticking to the theme of Kafka's deep connection with the fate of German culture in general.

---

*And with meta-hindsight, who's to say Kafka was wrong in wanting Germany and Austria to win the Great War? The Empires of Hohenzollern and Habsburg, triumphant, enlarged and practically conjoined, would no doubt have been very irksome things for many people west of the Rhine, south of the Alps, north of the Channel and especially east of the Danube. But they would certainly never have decided to exterminate their Jewish citizens.

IV

THE STAGES OF THE MYTH

Franz Kafka, der für seine Erzählun-
gen „Der Heizer" und „Die Verwandlung" den
Fontane-Preis erhielt

On June 11, 1918, with the Germans shelling Paris itself,
Kafka is so unknown that he gets three mentions on a
single page of the *Prague Daily News*. His Fontane
Prize, virtually ignored by modern biographers,
is still thought worth noting two-and-a-half years
after the event.

Myth 1: Kafka Was Almost Unknown in His Lifetime (Partly Because He Was So Fastidiously Shy About Publishing)

In general terms, the myth of the great artist ignored in his life-time is just that—a myth.[1] It's simply a fantasy that we *want* to be true—and like all sentimentality, it's merely the flip side of something deeply unattractive. Reading about our dead idols having been poor, lonely and disregarded is merely the soft-centered cousin of our sneaky wish to read about our living idols being caught with their pants down, their nostrils caked with white or their partners cheating.

I hope that the first chapter of this book will have pretty well knocked the notion on the head as far as Kafka's concerned, but it's such a basic part of the K.-myth that it's vital to get this straight. After all, the standard German reference work, *Franz Kafka: Eine Chronik* still claims on its cover that he was "almost unknown in his lifetime"; most biographers of Kafka, people who have presumably spent years studying the facts, still repeat some version of the sentimental drivel that "like many great writers, he was never to know that he was a great writer" (Hayman); and Britain's top Kafka-scholar recently praised Germany's top Kafka-scholar for arguing against "the notion, still common today, that Kafka was scarcely noted by colleagues and reviewers."[2]

So let's say it loudly and clearly: *the idea that Kafka was virtually unknown in his lifetime is nonsense.*

He did not die an already *famous* writer in international terms, of course, nor did he die rich. But we get some idea of how much the media-folk of his own city knew and liked him when we see him named three times in two entirely different articles in a single edition of the *Prague Daily News* (June 11, 1918). And we can get some idea of how he was professionally regarded beyond Prague if we recall that in early 1918 he was cold-called by two rival publishers who wanted to tempt him away from Kurt Wolff & Co.

So what happened to let people ever begin to think that Kafka was unknown and obscure? The answer, as so often, lies not in Kafka's personal life, nor in his alleged psychology, but in the wider world about him. We can clearly see this if we look at the history of his matchless short story volume *A Country Doctor.*

When the Going Was Good

By summer 1917, Kafka's career was quietly gathering speed, no doubt much helped by the Fontane Prize affair. At thirty-four, he now had four books out: *Meditation*, *The Stoker, The Metamorphosis*, and his beloved "The Judgment." All had been widely and very well reviewed. The stunning fable "Before the Law" was out there, too. *The Metamorphosis* had already had enough impact for a bizarre homage-cum-sequel (*The Metamorphosis Back of Gregor Samsa*) to have been published by one of Werfel's hangers-on.

With his ever-loyal little sister Ottla's ancient, tiny house providing the perfect silent yet friendly semi-home for his writing,

Kafka had written an entire volume's worth of short stories over the winter and spring of 1916/17. Of them, "Jackals and Arabs" and the brilliant "Report for an Academy" had already appeared in magazine form.

Herr Kurt Wolff had meanwhile been excused from his wartime duties, thanks to the intervention of a very influential friend (the Prince of Hessen) and allowed to return to more profitable battles on behalf of German culture.

On July 3, 1917, Wolff wrote that he'd heard about Kafka's "new works" from Brod (of course) and asked Kafka to send them to him, typed out. Four days later, Kafka did so. Within two weeks, Wolff had written back, offering to publish. On the twenty-seventh, Kafka accepted and said that he hoped he could rely on Wolff's support after the war, when he expected to marry, move to Berlin, and support himself solely by writing. On August 1, Wolff replied from his vacation resort that Kafka could count on his "ongoing material support."

So: from Wolff's first request to see the works via his agreement to publish to his fulsome avowals of future support took less than a month in total, even with each letter or package having to cross wartime frontiers at wartime speeds during the summer vacation. If it still needs saying: this isn't the way a reticent author acts, or how an unregarded author is treated.

We shouldn't be led astray by the fact that Kafka was (briefly) hesitant about publishing "In the Penal Colony" at this time. This doesn't show that Kafka was a holy man of meticulousness (and so on). It simply shows that he could *afford to be* hesitant about anything he thought less than up to standard—and perhaps that he felt he *should* be hesitant.

"In the Penal Colony," after all, had got him his worst-ever reviews when he read it publicly in Munich in November 1916. The whole thing, Kafka wrote to Felice, was, "a genuinely mighty failure." The poet Rilke, while very kind, had said that neither this story nor *The Metamorphosis* had equalled the older *The Stoker*.

And far worse, one Munich reviewer had called Kafka, flat out and in print, "a lecher of horror."

Reading this review by a man who didn't have (as we do) insider knowledge of the disturbing images in Kafka's diaries (butchers' knives slicing him up, feeding himself bit by bit to dogs, and so on) or of what he'd kept in his locked bookcase, Kafka may well have felt that it was an uncomfortably insightful warning against letting the Policeman of the Unconscious get too lax. After all, even the ever-flattering Wolff, house publisher of the avant-garde, admitted that he found the content hard to take.

Why rush things? Kafka was comfortably off (war bonds and all), one day he would inherit, and he had been assured—in black and white—that he could count on the "ongoing material support" of his friendly millionaire publisher if and when he ever actually got around to giving up his cushy day job and trying his luck as a writer in Berlin. Having prevailed on Felice (again) to marry him after the war (they had spent a surprisingly successful holiday at Marienbad together in 1916, when—as far as we can tell—they had finally made love) he was not even looking down the dreaded barrel of bachelor loneliness any more. With his stock clearly rising and his future seemingly assured, why risk blowing it by being overhasty in letting out a story that had been so cooly received. Why not try to find a better ending for "In the Penal Colony," for example, or maybe any kind of ending for the splendid "Great Wall of China," while the new collection of stories got out there and kept his name warm?

That was the way Franz Kafka's world was in 1917 as July turned into August: it was looking pretty good, and there seemed to be no great need to hurry.

The Bonfire of the Promises

Kafka (not, in fact, being blessed with paranormal abilities) had no idea in late July 1917 that, within a few days, he would find himself coughing up blood and that, within fourteen months, many kinds of promises, however written down in black and white, would look very hollow, indeed.

As it turned out, 1917 was the last full year of Kafka's Prague. If he had been lucky in his choice of friends and publishers (and in his own privileged life) up until late summer, he was as unlucky as the rest of German culture in the six and a half years that followed.

Ludendorff's great 1918 offensive, the Kaiser-Battle, failed, as did every great offensive on the Western Front, although it came closer than any other to succeeding. Despite innovative tactics and great early successes, Germany was unable to break the Allies. For once, Britain's "lions led by donkeys" actually had the technological edge, in the shape of the world's first massed tanks. And the Americans at last made their limitless manpower felt on the battlefield.

Germany and Austria lost, to the utter shock of their populations who, unbombed, uninvaded, and untroubled by a free press, had been fed black-and-white promises of victory (and maps of vast conquests) right up to the last minute.

Kafka's investment in war bonds was wiped out, a financial catastrophe he shared with millions of hard-working, hard-saving, government-trusting Austrians and Germans. Having been diagnosed with TB in 1917, he fell dangerously ill in October 1918 with the Spanish flu, which killed almost a quarter of a million people in Germany alone. He was bedridden and semiconscious for weeks, with a temperature spiking at nearly 106 degrees (enough for instant hospitalization today), during the days when German-speaking, German-Jewish Prague became history.

Western Europeans and Americans think of the Great War as ending in November 1918. But for Middle and Eastern Europeans, the armistice merely ushered in years of revolution, counterrevolution, hyperinflation, border-redrawing, and turmoil. Bohemian Germans tried to become part of Austria and found themselves under Czech military occupation. Newly independent Poles and

German *Freikorps* fought entire miniature campaigns. Budapest and Munich had short-lived Bolshevik dictatorships, while Trotsky's Red Army itself was only stopped by the "miracle of the Vistula." With the collapse of the imperial dynasties, all Mitteleuropa seemed up for grabs. Romanians, Hungarians, Bulgarians, Serbians, Czechs, and Poles all tried to sneak de facto control of disputed territories from Russia, Germany, Austria, and one another before Wilson, Lloyd George, and Clemenceau could agree on the final shape of the new order.

In a world where emperors could be dethroned (even killed) and where legal bonds drawn on ancient states could be rendered entirely worthless overnight, it's hardly surprising that fulsome but noncontractual avowals of loyalty from one's publisher should not turn out to be very valuable, either.

It's worth (as his beloved Kleist might have put it) carving this fact in brass: *Kafka's prospects as a German writer changed drastically—as did Prague's, as did Europe's—between July 1917 and November 1918.*

Wanting a Novel

The material effects of the defeat can be seen in the history of "A Country Doctor." In 1917, Wolff had been highly enthusiastic, but end-of-war and postwar chaos meant that basic things, including printing paper, typeface bronze, and reliable colleagues, were almost impossible to get hold of. The book was delayed again and again. According to Brod, Kafka was so angry at the setbacks that he actually wrote a (lost) letter of ultimatum to Wolff & Co. in 1918—which may not fit the icon of Saint Kafka, but certainly seems believable when we think back to the tone of the Fontane Prize letter in October 1915.

If Kafka felt things needed hurrying along, he was right. Three years can be a long time in a writer's career, one in which many doors meant only for him can close. By 1920, when "A Country Doctor" finally made it out, the German-speaking culture within which Kafka lived and wrote had suffered its unthinkable, epochal defeat.

Kurt Wolff was still keen to publish him, but the urbane millionaire of swaggering imperial Germany was now a man who—understandably—saw hard postwar times a-coming in the new and still unstable Weimar Republic. Wolff's letter of October 3, 1921, which can seem like a man practically begging his author for more material, has to be read in the light of how publishers *do* talk to their writers. Under all the old-fashioned effusive politeness and respect (which, of course, cost nothing), there is clearly brewing—as Kafka the lawyer must have seen—an ultimatum whose real meaning is something like:

> Look, times are hard, the public wants novels; if you publish a novel maybe the short stories will sell. Brod has told us you've got two novels, so how about showing them to us? We love your stuff and we hope one day the German reading public will catch up, but how can you expect us to keep on pushing an author who doesn't sell and who doesn't seem to care if he sells or not?

Was this letter—the longest Wolff ever wrote to him—anything to do with Kafka's decision, less than four months later, to once more try writing a novel after years without having written even a major short story? With any other writer we might well consider the possibility, so perhaps we should do so here.

At any rate, Kafka did *not* have a novel ready to give Wolff in October 1921 and, by now, his life was genuinely in the crisis he had mentally pictured back in 1911–14. It was no longer a question of choices and dilemmas and evasions and dreams: it had come down to life and death. He was seriously ill, was about to hand over his diaries to Milena (either as a last desperate gambit to win her or as an admission that it was all over), and had written hardly a thing for four years.

By the time the often murderous chaos in and around Germany finally ceased, Kafka was done for. On the day Adolf Hitler walked into Landsberg Castle to begin his grotesquely and fatally light sentence (a single year of gentleman-like imprisonment for having tried to take over the government of Germany by armed force), Franz Kafka had only two months left before he died a few score miles away.

In short, in the years when Kafka might otherwise have been reaping the benefits of his growing reputation, people in the German-speaking world often had rather more pressing things on their minds (and budgets) than books. As Brod wrote on January 1, 1921, "In Berlin, all the writers are fleeing into steady jobs and the civil service . . . serious literature is bankrupt."

During Kafka's final two years, as Europe hesitantly returned to something like life, the signs were positive. When he sent "A Hunger Artist" to Germany's top cultural journal and his own long time read, the *New Review* (which had been distinctly un-bowled over by *The Metamorphosis*), it was immediately accepted and swiftly published. When Wolff & Co. finally closed his account, he had no trouble getting a new publisher—and a decent advance—for his next collection of stories.

Kafka was still in there, still writing and being published, still backed, but like many other writers with roots deep in the lost, pre-war world, he was going to need time to adjust to the radically new, postwar realities.

His clock was just ticking too fast. Like Germany and Austria, he had been riding high in the summer of 1917, but then he had gotten very unlucky indeed.

Even so, Kafka died in the saddle, correcting the proofs of the book he knew would soon come out, a pretty, vivacious, and devoted young actress at his side. He also knew that he had been hailed by most of the major German writers of his day—fellow-authors such as Robert Musil (who wanted to publish him), Rainer Maria Rilke (who followed his development with great interest), Carl Sternheim (who had handed him that publicity coup), Georg Kaiser (who visited him in person while in Prague) and Hermann Hesse (who had drawn the public's attention to Kafka more than once). He could be certain that his work had the active backing of many then influential figures in the literary world—such men as Werfel, Weiss, Weltsch, Ehrenstein, Pick, Blei, Tucholsky, and of course the tireless, successful, and well-connected Brod.

Many writers would kill to die knowing themselves to be so unknown and unregarded. Except of course, Kafka didn't *want* his work to survive him, he wanted it destroyed.

Didn't he?

Well, let's see.

Myth 2: Kafka Wanted His Works Destroyed After His Death

This is a basic plank of the K.-myth as told to tourists in Prague—and as taught in most colleges.

Kafka actually wrote two short wills. The first one was undated, written in ink, folded, and addressed to Brod, who found it among the papers in Kafka's writing desk. It read as follows:

Dearest Max, my last wish: Everything that I leave behind in the way of diaries, manuscripts, letters of my own and from others, drawing, etc. (whether in my bookcase, clothes cupboard, writing desk at home or at the office, or in any other place anything may have gotten and you find it) should be burned, completely and unread, as should everything written or drawn in your possession or in the possession of others whom you should ask, in my name, to do likewise. People who do not want to hand over letters to you should at least be made to promise that they themselves will burn them.

Yours, Franz Kafka

The second one was dated November 29 (yearless, but even rival scholars have agreed: 1922) and was found by Brod "on closer examination" of the leftover papers:

Dear Max, This time I really might not get up again, a pulmonary infection is probable enough after this month of fever and even the fact that I write it down won't keep it away, though the act has a certain power.

So in this case my last wish regarding everything of my writings is as follows:

Out of all I have written, only the following books count: Judgment, Stoker, Metamorphosis, Penal Colony, Country Doctor and the story Hunger Artist. (The few copies of Meditation can be left alone, I don't want to give anyone the trouble of treading them into the ground, but it mustn't be reprinted.) When I say that these five books and one story count, I don't mean that I have any wish that they be reprinted and preserved for future times; on the contrary, if they should be completely lost, this would be in accordance with my real wishes. It's simply that, their being already there, I don't stand in the way of anyone keeping them alive if he feel like it.

On the other hand, everything else that exists in the way of my writings (publications in journals, manuscripts and letters) is *without exception* inasmuch as it's possible to get hold of it or to ask from it from the addressees (you know most of them anyway, it mainly concerns Frau Felice M., Frau Julie née Wohryzeck and Frau Milena Pollak, especially don't forget the few notebooks that Frau Pollak

has)—all this is, *without exception and preferably unread* (I don't actually forbid you to look at them, though I'd prefer you not to, at any
rate no one else may look at them)—all this, without exception, is to
be burned and you are asked to do this as quickly as possible by me,
Franz

There have been volumes of wonderful stuff written about
these notes. The coeditor of the new facsimile Kafka edition,
Roland Reuss waxes theoretical about them his introduction, going well beyond any student-revue parody of Teutonic exactitude
and professorial cunning. His argument, in a much shortened version, runs something like this:

> Kafka's first note said that he wanted all the writings (and drawings)
> he left behind to be burned unread. But aha! Kafka is playing a
> fiendishly clever game! Max Brod only knew this *because he had read
> the note*, and since the note logically forms *part* of the writing Kafka
> left behind, this means that Brod only ever got the order to burn
> everything *because he hadn't done so.* He had already—he *had to have*
> already—defied the order to burn everything even before he ever got
> it! How Kafkaesque: a man is given an order but the way he gets the
> order means the order *can never* be obeyed! And then, of course, the
> existence of the second note completely undermines this, because
> how can one have *two* "last wills"? And doesn't a pencil-written doc-
> ument, that will fade with time naturally, positively *invite* the idea of
> corrections?

Which begs the question how Kafka could ever have left *any*
written will instructing *anyone* to do *anything* without this professor falling over himself to theorize it out of existence. No doubt, if
Kafka had typed out his instructions, we would by now have
goodly academic acres of stuff on the *special nature of mechanical*

writing in Kafka's mind and so on. But in a laughably roundabout way, Reuss is perfectly correct.

There's no doubt at all that Kafka didn't mean a word of it. Of course he didn't, and the fact that he took so long—so almost comically long—to get to the actual verb ('burned') in his second will is only a little giveaway.

Kafka was a lawyer. He knew very well what a binding legal document looked like and that neither of these supposed wills was remotely a real one. Brod claims that he'd even told Kafka flat out, at the time of the first will, that he wouldn't carry out the instructions. And in fact (although Reuss relegates it to a footnote, despite his professional obsession with acts of writing), Kafka actually *had it in writing* that Brod was psychologically ready to take over as step-author—and implicitly believed himself able to do it. On August 1, 1919, Brod wrote to Kafka (jokingly, of course, but in writing) that since Wolff & Co. wanted novels, not more short stories, "I'll knock your *Trial* into shape with my own hands."*

So there really is no need for endless theoretical word dissection here. As always, things get far simpler if we forget the icon and, for once, just try to treat Kafka as a normal human being with normal thought processes (what *other* kind of thought processes is he supposed to have had, for God's sake?).

Brod had put an ethereal, artistic figure based on Kafka in a book as early as 1904. He'd pushed Kafka's name on the world in 1907 before Kafka had ever published a word. And he'd kept pushing ever since. By entrusting Brod of all people with collecting and destroying his writing (and by helpfully telling him exactly where to find it and from whom to get it), Kafka knew very well that he was doing the best thing possible to make sure it was preserved and broadcast.

---

*Brod's original German was even more muscular. A literal translation would be: "I'll cut your *Trial* to an end on my own fist."

In doing so, he was merely acting the way he'd acted in every field of his life: maneuvring someone else into making the big decisions, to keep up the fiction (which seems to have been vital to his sense of himself) that he was a man without intentions, a mere plaything of other people's desires (meaning that he could never be held guilty for the results).*

There's really no doubt: when Kafka instructed Brod to destroy his work, he didn't for one moment expect it to happen. And he was right, of course.

Thanks to Brod, we have the stories Kafka published in his lifetime *and* the stories he didn't. In some ways, it would be better if that were *all* we had, because it would have prevented much of the K.-myth from ever growing. For example, if the stories were all we had, it would surely never have occurred to people to claim that Kafka's Jewishness is vital to understanding his writing.

Myth 3: Kafka's Jewishness Is Vital to Understanding His Writing

If we knew nothing of Kafka but his fiction, published and unpublished, the only decisive evidence that this unknown genius was Jewish would be the fact that, from 1915 onward, many of his stories came out first in journals published by Jewish editors for Jewish readers (before being published in book form by gentiles).

Even then, knowing nothing else about him, we might doubt *how* Jewish this author was, because only one little unfinished story—about a strange creature that lives in "our synagogue"—actually has a narrator or hero who is Jewish, and even here the

---

*Alt sees this psychology as central to Kafka's whole life—he wanted to remain an apparently innocent "eternal son" (as opposed to a grown man). Writing of Kafka's behavior during his engagement, Stach agrees: "It is disconcerting—especially to readers determined to see Kafka in the best possible light—how he tried to shirk his responsibility in critical situations by leaving matters in other people's hands." Kafka's *stories*, of course, are totally aware that this evasion cannot work.

word is never used. Whereas in other, far more prominent places (the family in *The Metamorphosis,* the Cathedral in *The Trial*) the setting is explicitly Christian.

In other words, very little in the actual writings should make us think—as so many critics have claimed—that, to understand these stories properly, we need to reach for our Torah or our Hassidic tales. What makes us think this is not anything in his *writings* but our knowledge of his *life.* It's perhaps the clearest example of people too busy looking at Kafka's life rather than at his writing.

Now, of course, Kafka was Jewish, he was very much aware of it, and, as he grew older, he became more and more so. He made himself reasonably fluent in Hebrew and flirted heavily with Zionism. He had never bought into the curative promises of psychoanalysis and, by the end of his life, had decided that trying to write the "dirt" out of himself was simply a yielding to "dark forces." In the life story of Kafka the man, yes, it certainly seems as if working out his relationship with his Judaism was the only thing that held out any hope of some therapeutic healing of his soul.

However, when we read of his touching Zionists dreams—to live in Palestine as a waiter or bookbinder—we should remember that his stories often know all about the temptingly warm visions of consolation that can come from the "grossly delusional perspective" of a man who has lost all real hope (this is how he described it in a letter to Felice of June 15, 1913). Kafka was very clearly a dying man when he considered these profound career changes, and how deeply his Zionism really went may be doubted, for he made no known comment at all on the Balfour Declaration, that epochal event to any serious campaigner for Israel.

It's clear Kafka was fascinated by the thought of a real life, one lived beyond the lonely tower of the ego, of class, of convention.

But everyone was, in his day. "O Mankind!" was the pathetic cry of the whole Expressionist Generation, and Kafka's work is very unusual at this time for examining the real *price* of belonging more than the supposed rewards.

The narrator of "The Great Wall of China" bursts into wonderful, unexpected lyricism when he describes feeling part of a vast, united population—but he also clearly reveals that the whole thing is artificially induced by the powers-that-be, and refuses to question further, in case he undermines society. In *The Castle,* K. longs to be accepted by the authorities, or at least (as he tires) by the village, but it's plain that the price of belonging is absolute, forelock-tugging conformism to a corrupt hierarchy.

Of course, Kafka often longed to belong. Everyone does. But his late dreams of a simple, nonliterary, hard-working life in a new homeland, Palestine, are rather like the dying Travis Bickle's vision of a down-home American paradise at the end of *Taxi Driver*: achingly warm, infinitely moving . . . and totally unreal.

The Tough Jew

Many writers have claimed that Kafka's obsession with his own (supposed) physical unfitness and weakness is a typical symptom of Jewish self-hatred and that this mirrors contemporary racist views of the Jews. They take this on to suggest that there is a specifically Jewish angle to Kafka's concerns with the physical body, punishment, and so on. This is tempting and apparently commonsense stuff, but when the same writers say (as they do, being of a biographical turn of mind) that Kafka's sense of his weakness was due to his awe of his father, it all starts to unravel.

Kafka thought of his father as man who was both more authentically Jewish and more of a man than was Kafka himself. Hermann was the archetypal Tough Jew. The son of a kosher butcher, he had made it up in the ranks of the German-speaking

Habsburg army until he reached *Zugführer,* roughly a British sergeant major or a U.S. staff sergeant, a rank of considerable day-to-day importance in any army and the highest an uneducated draftee could attain in his three years' service. Kafka as a boy (according to himself) shivered in Hermann's shadow at the pool; had to listen to his endless tales of extreme physical hardship in the shtetl; looked on with dismay as Czech employees were bawled out and humiliated; choked with laughter at his comic performances of Jewish rituals on high days; and sat baffled round the table as Jews, Czechs, and Germans were all denounced as idiots, one lot after the other, just as the feeling took him. There was no sign whatever of the insecure intellectual about Hermann Kafka.

So if Kafka's father, an utterly assimilationist yet undeniably Jewish tough guy, was Kafka's touchstone for ruthless self-assertion, it's very hard to see how Kafka would have arrived at the notion that Jewish males as such (and hence, himself *as* a Jewish male) were physically weak and somehow inherently contemptible. This circle just won't square.

It would be truer to argue that Kafka felt somehow weakened by his *lack* of authentic Jewishness, but this is artificially ghettoizing the Jewish experience. Every thinking man in Europe, whether of Catholic, Protestant, or Jewish background, was facing up to the implications of Darwinism and of Nietzsche's "Death of God." Many of them, like Kafka (and like almost every conservative thinker since), linked this philosophical crisis to unhealthy modern city life.

Kafka's obsession with making his body more "healthy" was not at all specifically Jewish. On the contrary, it was hugely fashionable. His exercise bible, *Mein System,* was a massive international bestseller, after all. When Kafka yearned for, and sweated near-naked for, a body like Müller's, he was pursuing a very common fantasy—that "modern man" was an unmanly, overintellectual, unattractive sort of city-dwelling creature (what Nietzsche called a "decadent") who scarcely knew what real life was anymore, and who could do with a bracing sea breeze or some cold mountain air, a bit of getting back to the soil, a dose of intellectual-cum-physical hardening and beautifying—by, for example, taking part in a decent war.

To see this fashionable (and eventually, for Europe, almost fatal) *intellectual self-hatred* only through the lens of Jewishness does not help open up Kafka's writing, but puts blinkers on it.

How to See What Is Not There

Still, it seems obvious that Kafka's Jewishness must have been important to his work in *some* way or other and, therefore, it's something we should study to enjoy that work the better. How could it fail to be? How could the fact that he belonged to a nation (or, as the killers would put it, a race) that would be foully hunted down in his part of the world less than twenty years after his death *not* be important?

This is the sort of thing pushed by a whole school of critics (mainly in America) who insist on bringing "heritage" into the work of every writer. To them, a black writer simply *must* be writing about his or her blackness, a Jewish writer about his or her Jewishness, a gay writer about his or her gayness, and so on. What else *would* they be writing about? Some of these so-called scholars have even said that people who don't share a certain "heritage" can't really appreciate the writing—and therefore can't critically discuss it. This is a handy way of making exclusive your academic job (or indeed creating it), but has pretty fatal implications for literature as a form of communication.

These critics deal with the fact that there is almost zero actual Jewishness in Kafka's work by saying that since *we* know Kafka was Jewish, this *must* mean that he is deliberately *repressing the Jewishness* of his narrators and heroes, mustn't it? Obviously.

Which means that his stories are *really* "about" this repression of Jewishness!

It will be, for anyone outside academe, almost incredible that educated and tenured people take this backward logic seriously, but I assure readers that they do. So let's test this way of arguing by applying it to the references in Kafka's writings to the conflict between the Czechs and the Germans.

There aren't any. But that's the whole point.

Kafka's stories very often have poor people in them. In *The Trial,* the Court is located in a poor suburb that Kafka at first describes realistically, much the same way as Dickens or Dostoyeysky might have done. In *The Castle,* the village is divided into a strict hierarchy with the senior officials at the top and the villagers at the bottom. In *The Metamorphosis,* there is much talk of the family's maids. Now, we know that in Kafka's Prague, the poor were always with him (even if they were only bringing him food and drink and sex) and we know that they were almost always Czech. In his writings, however, the many poor people his heroes run across are, as far as we can tell, every bit as German as the heroes themselves.

But the German-Czech conflict was something Kafka *must* have been made aware of every single day of his conscious life, in some way or another. We know that he was, for a German, unusually nondismissive of Czech language and culture. So if this conflict has no explicit echoes anywhere in his work, if Kafka *didn't* write about poor people as Czechs, ever, he must have been *permanently repressing* this vital social factor, mustn't he? Which means that his writings are thus all actually *about* the German-Czech conflict after all, doesn't it?

See what nonsense this is? So let's suggest another answer. Perhaps Kafka *chose* not to highlight his Jewishness in his writings and *chose* not to color them with the German-Czech conflicts of his native city. Perhaps he made these choices because he had the first skill needed by any writer: to know the difference between what's important *to yourself* and what's important *to your story*.

We (obsessed as we are with belonging and identity) may imagine that to Kafka, his being Jewish must have been an absolutely central and decisive part of his life and therefore of his writing. But what Kafka actually said again and again was that his being *a writer* was the most important thing about his life. As far as identity went, he thought of his "blood relatives" as some of the biggest guns of European literature.

"This will never make it beyond Bodenbach," was the crushing reaction of the much-envied Franz Werfel on first reading Kafka's stuff—by which Werfel meant that Kafka's early writing was fatally provincial. Whether Kafka was ever told, or tactfully warned at second hand, about what the then great Werfel had said, we'll never know, but we do know that Kafka wanted his works to resonate. He took considerable care about where they were placed, how they looked, what the reviewers said about them. From 1915 onward, he decided that many of them might best appear in publications aimed specifically at German-speaking Jews who, of course, were not simply German-speaking Jews, but were among Europe's leading intellectual groups. But the rest of the time— certainly, when writing the works he's best remembered for—he was writing for an audience way beyond Bodenbach.

That audience was the audience of Goethe (who almost obsessed him at times), of Kleist (whose *Anecdotes* he wanted his first book to physically look like), of Flaubert (whose *Sentimental Education* he adored), of Dickens (of whom *Amerika* was, he said, "pure imitation") of Dostoyevsky (whose long-dead features Kafka knew well enough to recognize them in a dream about Milena). *That* audience—the audience of pan-European literature—neither knew nor cared a jot what Prague Germans/Jews and Prague Czechs were arguing about in their provincial little coffeehouse hothouse. And nor, when he was writing for them, as he certainly was completely until after giving up on *The Trial*, did Kafka. Which is perhaps why he didn't use those elements in his stories.

In other words, Kafka's writing doesn't *repress* what he inescapably *was* (a Jew)—it *expresses* what he clearly wished *to become* (part of German and European literature).

Which he has, of course. But sadly, not in the way he should have. This is because of the next myth.

Myth 4: Kafka's Style Is Mysterious and Opaque

This is the easiest myth of all to dismiss but the hardest to cure.

In his lifetime, Kafka was known for "absolutely the purest and clearest German prose anyone is writing today."* The odd reviewer who didn't like a particular story much still admitted his storytelling talent: *New Review*'s lukewarm piece on *The Metamorphosis* had to praise Kafka's "clean, unromantic storytelling" and even his worst-ever reviewer, Otto Hesse on "In the Penal Colony," mentioned Kafka's "strong gift for storytelling."

This may come as news to readers used to *their* Kafka sounding like some ghastly, plodding sub-Sartre.

And why does he sound like this in translation? Because this is what the translators all subconsciously think he *should* sound like. And why do Kafka's translators think this? Because (like everyone else) they come to his writing not innocently, but already trailing the fatal clouds of the ready-made K.-myth.

It's hard enough for Germans to escape the K.-myth, but at least Germans have the clean, beautiful originals to read if they can bear to take off their gloom-tinted biographical spectacles. Kafka's translators have made it almost impossible for anyone else.

---

*Said Kurt Tucholsky, another fellow-writer who liked Kafka personally (they got on so well at their first meeting on 30th September 1911 that they went off together to Prague's poshest brothel) and later gave him thumpingly good reviews.

The only hope here is that some publishing tycoon with the fabled "Button A" on his or her desk will press it to commission genuinely new translations that will at last truly speak to his millions of English-speaking readers.

Many of whom are now doubtlessly reading their Kafka in lonely little apartments in cities where they know hardly anyone, consoling themselves with the next myth . . .

Myth 5: Kafka Was Poor and Lonely, or Free, and Thereby Lost

The Kafka industry is surely to blame for many young and creative people foolishly embarking on a life of modern, metropolitan purgatory. After all, look what Kafka achieved! And Kafka was intense and lonely, too, wasn't he?

Well, not in the way we think of it, he wasn't. Other writers at the time were describing the struggling artist lost in a modern, noisy, low-rent urban world (Rilke's *Malte Laurids Brigge* is the greatest example) but Kafka's life was nothing remotely like this.

Kafka lived in his family's apartment until 1914 (when he was thirty-one), then was more or less kicked out to make room for his sister and her kids. Where did he go? Into his sister's vacant flat, of course—then into his *other* sister's flat. He finally moved to his own place (in the same street as one of his sisters) in February 1915. Even then, he continued to eat at home almost every day. In the winter of 1916/17, he did his writing in his youngest sister's tiny hideaway cottage (sometimes she brought him his dinner there). In early 1917, he did finally rent a place at some remove from his family, across the river from the Old Town, but it was no garret. It was a high-ceilinged set of big rooms in what's now the U.S. embassy. When his TB was diagnosed in August, he moved back in with his parents, then out to the country, to his sister Ottla's, where he spent eight months. He then moved back in with his parents, alternating thereafter between their home, semi-sanatorium hotels (which were very common in TB-ridden Old Europe), and later actual medical sanatoriums until his last, brief vain move to Berlin with his third fiancée.

As for poverty, it was something he never knew until the whole of Germany got to know it in the blackest of the postwar years. Before this, he took his vacations and cures in hotels and sanatoria frequented by senior army officers and the like. In 1918, his father bought a large apartment building in central Prague outright as an investment for his retirement: it cost 500,000 crowns at a time when Kafka was earning about 6,500 a year, and a Czech working man about 1,000. You can do the comparative social arithmetic yourself. And *then* Hermann sold his business. This is why, when Kafka did at last come to taste real poverty as a retired man on a fixed pension whose value was wiped out by hyperinflation, his parents could and did still help him out.

In other words, he spent the vast majority of his adult life *anything but* physically alone and poor. He spent it in a city where, as we've already seen, he was completely part of a tight-knit middle-class minority where he knew (and was known to) everyone who mattered. His work involved all sorts of incessant contact with colleagues; in 1912, his breakthrough year as a writer, the pace of his social life, as we can see from his diaries, was downright hectic.

Of course, this isn't to say that Kafka didn't *feel* isolated. You can *feel* horribly alone in a crowded party. But Kafka's "loneliness" was nothing remotely to do with *actual physical solitude*. It was the feeling of a man surrounded by other people, many of whom he had every reason to be close to, yet who found himself unable to *connect* with the stream of human traffic all around him (as his contemporary, E. M. Forster, put it).

True physical loneliness was something that Kafka may have fantasized about needing, but for all the noise he made about the unbearable racket at home, on the very rare occasions when his family proposed to actually leave him alone in his supposedly longed-for total peace—over the Whitsun weekend of 1912, for example—the twenty-nine-year old Kafka was filled with simple "angst" (*Diary*, May 23, 1912).

He would not be the first writer to fantasize about being utterly free to write and then find he can't bear the physical and mental silence. After his illness struck and he finally dissolved his second engagement to Felice, Kafka was finally faced with the real prospect of loneliness. He viewed it with loathing.

Even his most adoring biographers find it hard to put any sort of heroic light on Kafka's engagement to (and dropping of) the penniless, uneducated, and ill Julie Wohryzeck. A few of them try to suggest that this shows how unbourgeois Kafka was, but that's pretty desperate stuff. When things look up—i.e., when it seems like there's a better offer in the alluring shape of stylish, much-desired Milena—Kafka is ruthless about Julie. He stays engaged to her while pursuing Milena by letter, simply calling her "the girl" in his letters to his new object of desire. There's a clear sense of utter confidence that he can have Julie or not, just as he pleases. It's almost as if he keeps a fiancée on the books simply as emotional ballast to even things up in his wooing of a married woman. And he doesn't actually burn his boats with Julie until he's sure (or thinks he's sure) that he's really got Milena.

Kafka seems to have known deep down that *freedom* in our modern individualistic sense was the last thing he actually needed. There's an insight into this in the strange little fragment that reads like a part of *The Trial*: a man is summoned by a mysterious jury and informed, "You are free—and that is why you are lost."

So young artistic types who—quite rightly—love Kafka's stuff shouldn't go and live in cheap rented rooms in cities where they have no family and friends. Or rather, they can do it if they want, but whether the experience of being poor and alone in a friendless city kills these young people or makes them stronger, it will be nothing whatever to do with anything Kafka ever experienced.

No, what Kafka knew was more like an eternal Christmas—as we'll now see.

Myth 6 : Kafka's Father Was Monstrous, or Christmas Never Ends

Imagine for a terrible moment that the wish in that hellish Christmas rock anthem comes true and it is suddenly *Christmas every day, forever.*

Your parents are there forever, your brothers and sisters (the unmarried ones) are there forever, and the married ones are always popping in and out. Your grandparents, if they are alive, are there forever, as well. Aunts and uncles come and go, nieces and nephews scream and play, forever. And since this is Christmas, forever, the dreaded laws of Christmas apply forever, too. You have to defer to your mother's cooking, your father's body clock, your grandmother's digestion, your grandfather's stories, your siblings' children's spoiledness—forever.

You have to give up your bedroom uncomplainingly if more family members arrive; spend evenings stuck inside, telling old stories and playing cards; go along to half-understood ceremonies in places of worship that bore you stupid; watch old movies on TV that you would never normally waste five minutes on. All forever.

Every day, you have to listen to your father's opinions on everything; *every day*, you have to nod at your mother's well-meaning but useless advice; *every day*, you have to see relatives or siblings or family friends you have no real reason to want to see, and to be jammed together with them with little hope of any personal space. If you have one locked bookcase that is genuinely respected as your own exclusive domain, you're lucky.

Of course, there is no written law of Christmas that says you have to do all these things. There doesn't have to be. You know it anyway. You just *have* to do all of this. You have to because, well, you just *have* to. Because you know that if you don't do these things you will be automatically punished, by yourself, without trial, by vast weights of guilt from *not having done the right thing*.

And even though it is all highly inconvenient for you personally, when the end of the day comes, when the last plate has been washed, the last quarrel patched up, the last child tucked in and the last elderly relative seen to bed, when you can at last have five minutes' peace on the balcony and maybe even take a stroll out for a nightcap, you feel that strange, warm, inexplicable Christmas glow that comes from knowing that you have done what the unwritten (but perfectly well-known) laws required of you. You have done well. You have done Christmas as it should be done.

And now you have to do it all again. Tomorrow and forever.

Christmas (plus Thanksgiving for Americans) is the only time when we modern Westerners feel anything like that sheer weight of Family. It's the only time each year when unwritten laws and customs really and truly still impinge on our treasured individual freedom to do just what we want whenever the hell we feel like it.

This makes the holiday season the only time of year that gives us any sort if insight into the powerful emotions of duty, guilt, and fulfillment that ran family life (which means: *life itself*, pretty much) for people in Kafka's day and continue to do so for the majority of people now alive on earth. Only at Christmas, to borrow one of Kafka's own images, do we grasp the fleeing coattails of real, old-fashioned family feelings.

No wonder that the season of goodwill is such a popular setting for our books and films—and no wonder we have such difficulty entering the mental worlds of our geopolitical opponents.

These, then, were the sort of social laws, unwritten but no less potent for that, which ruled family life in Kafka's time, day in, day out, all year round, forever.

There was no escape but marriage. No one moved out to live alone unless he or she was leaving their home town, period, either out of ambition or shame. Why would someone move out to live *alone?* This question, that seems so ridiculous to us now, would have seemed equally ridiculous (but the other way around) in Kafka's day.*

For example, when Kafka met Felice Bauer "at Max's," that actually meant at *Max's parents'*, which is where Max Brod (naturally) lived until he got married. The entire panoply of coffeehouses and late-night bars (and of course, *chambres séparées*) existed because people needed (and were prepared to pay for) somewhere they could go to escape the family for a while.

These worlds of eternal Christmas were ruled by fathers—again, not by any written law but by unbreakable custom. Which brings us, of course, to one of literary biography's greatest villains, Kafka's father.

Kafka in Bad Company Again

Few men who were never convicted of any crime have been so thoroughly pilloried as Hermann Kafka. The standard accounts of Kafka's life make him seem an unfeeling brute who so efficiently terrorized his only son, treating him practically like an insect, as to make him permanently lacking in self-confidence, fatally unfit for adulthood.

And yet, hold on. What are all these accounts based on? The (supposedly) autobiographical testimony of Kafka himself.

Hermann Kafka was a real man, not a story. So we should be

---

*And still does in many parts of the world. You can always tell when you are in one of these parts of the world by one infallible test: there will be *no launderettes.*

aware that in his case, the chief—the only—witness for the prosecution is Kafka himself, a master manipulator of language and image. Before we merely accept that unsupported accusation as actual fact, it should be examined rather more closely than heretofore.

To start with, we should know that in Kafka's day, it was practically de rigueur for literary artists to depict bold Artistic Sons struggling against uncomprehending, unfeeling, disciplinarian Bourgeois Fathers.

As the narrow conventions (and smug certainties) of the Victorian era gave way to the excitements and challenges of the vast modern world, virtually every artist of Kafka's time—the Expressionist Generation as they're now known—treated the theme of Sons and Fathers. Many of them were inspired by Nietzsche's declaration that what people call "morality" is simply *custom* made into holy writ.

Fathers were the embodiment of this false morality, this *morality of custom.* They didn't rule by any written or official or rational law, so there was no appeal that could be made against them. They ruled simply by the built-in virtue of being what they were: *fathers.* All that *sons* could do was to oppose the fatherly will with their *own* willpower, in a pure power struggle.

Here's one German-speaking artist of the Expressionist Generation describing the moment he revealed his artistic calling to his loyal Habsburg father. He's writing five years after Kafka wrote the famous "Letter to His Father." Just like Kafka, he looks back on his youth in the last century and vengefully immortalizes his father as a tyrannical Kaiser-era brute, a small-minded man with no understanding of his son's yearning to escape the spiritual death of a proposed civil-service career, of his longing for a life as a free artist.

So long as my father's intention that I should become a civil servant only came up against my own theoretical distaste for this profession, the conflict was bearable. Up to then, I was able to keep my private opinions to myself to some extent and did not always have to contradict him immediately. My own firm inner determination never to become a civil servant was enough for me. And that decision was adamantine. The problem came to a head when I developed a plan of my own that opposed my father's. [. . .] When I was first asked what I myself wanted to be, after once again rejecting my father's favorite plan, I rather abruptly blurted out the decision I had made. My father was struck speechless for few moments:

"A painter? An artist?"

He doubted my sanity, or perhaps he thought had heard wrongly or misunderstood. But when he realized how things were, and especially when he felt the seriousness of my intention, he opposed it with all the determination of his nature. This was an easy decision for him, since any consideration of whatever abilities I might really have was simply out of the question.

"An artist? No, never, as long as I live!"

Step forward once again . . . Adolf Hitler.

Hitler, that paragon of intellectual mediocrity and low political cunning, was aware that by portraying himself as a young "artistic" man in conflict with an old-fashioned, Victorian, bourgeois father, he could make himself seem "modern" and "radical." In other words, even someone as semiliterate as Hitler clearly knew that this theme of father-son conflict was an important part of the *Zeitgeist*. He also clearly saw that to present himself as a son frustrated in his choice of school, career, and so on by his old-fashioned, conformist father was a useful way of giving an entirely false dramatic arc to his own life story (which was one of entire failure until 1914, though of course, being by now a would-be German Mussolini, Hitler is careful to present it as a series of secret victories-in-waiting).

So if Hitler wrote like that about *his* father . . .

Two brutal and conformist Habsburg-era fathers with
artistically inclined sons they did not understand: Herman Kafka and Alois Hitler.

Hermann the Terrible?

The "Letter to His Father" is quoted at length in every book on Kafka, usually as if it's a simple and objective statement of auto-biographical fact. In it, Kafka blames his failures in life entirely on his inability to cope with the pressures of his father's expectations and his tyrannical character.

Even where there are bald facts that Kafka has to acknowledge—for example, the (at the time unusual) freedom he was given to study whatever he wanted in college (at his father's expense), he maintains that this wasn't really the gift of freedom it seemed because (a) Hermann was only following the value judgments of the Jewish middle class and (b) Hermann had by then so crushed him that he was incapable of caring what he did.

In this document filled (as Kafka admitted to Milena) with "lawyerly tricks," leading questions, and notional exchanges in which Kafka puts words into his father's mouth simply so that he can then refute them, what Kafka is essentially asking is that his father accept the fundamental blame for everything that has gone wrong in his life, so that they can both "live and die more easily."

It is an extraordinarily modern letter that could come straight from our own age of blame culture and obsession with childhood "abuse" as an excuse for failing to take responsibility for our lives. However, unlike in most such cases, in Kafka's we can access information that was never meant to be known by anyone else.

We can, in other words, objectively test Kafka's recall.

In Which Hermann Kafka Has No Idea of His Son's Nightlife

One of the most-quoted parts of the "Letter to His Father" is the one that is extraordinarily like the scene Kafka described in "The Judgment" six years before.* Here, Kafka records his father's earthy scorn of his third fiancée, the penniless Julie Wohryzek.

> She probably pulled on some carefully chosen blouse, the way Prague Jewesses know how to, and you? You naturally decided to marry her on the spot. And as quickly as possible, in a week, tomorrow, today. I just don't understand you. You're a grown man, you live in the city, yet you can't think of anything else to do except marry the first girl who comes along. Aren't there any other *possibilities*? If you're scared of that sort of place, I'll come with you.

It certainly sounds pretty harsh and unfeeling: a worldly father mocking his weak and sensitive son for being so sexually desperate that he'll marry anyone, suggesting he go to a brothel instead, and even mockingly offering to go along with him and hold his hand!

Rough stuff, and it seems quite understandable that Kafka should be shocked and hurt by his father's straightforward talk— although his own later treatment of Julie (he cheated on her se-

---

*It is this kind of thing that leads Alt to see a unique relationship between Kafka's writing and his life. Kafka writes about crises in his head which (because the writing never leads to any escape-route) will at some time inevitably be played out in reality. This gives the uncanny impression that Kafka's writings somehow predict his own life-disasters.

cretly and swiftly dumped her as soon as he thought he'd won Milena) was scarcely honorable. But there's a problem here.

Kafka and brothels? Remember? Kafka was a regular habitué of bordellos—indeed, it seems that he was at times almost uncontrollably drawn to them. So when Kafka takes this high-minded tone of distaste for his father's sergeants' mess talk of prostitutes, we should think twice.

Let's consider the position carefully. Are we to take Kafka's depiction of what his father said as *factually true* or not? And what are the consequences for the Case Against Hermann Kafka?

If Hermann Kafka *didn't* really say what his son *says* he said, it means that Kafka's famous letter is at heart simply a fabrication—case dismissed.

But if Hermann Kafka *did* really say all that, it means that Kafka must have been carefully concealing his nightlife from his father in all the years he lived with him—as carefully as he concealed his secret collection of pornography and his secret bank account.

Which means that we can scarcely blame Hermann Kafka for not having a deep understanding of his son's emotional needs.

Hermann the Liberal

In the letter, the most striking part, among all the accusations, is Kafka's admission that "you hardly once actually hit me." Note the words: *hardly once actually.* In a letter of such incessant accusation, we can reasonably take this to mean: *virtually never.*

Now, even if Hermann Kafka *did* hit Franz every now and then (which is the worst interpretation we can put on Kafka's words), that would hardly be much to write home about. We're talking about Queen Victoria's time, for heaven's sake. An ex-staff sergeant who did *not* use physical punishment on his male children simply as an everyday recourse was extremely rare in the nineteenth century (and for many decades afterward). It would be a century after Kafka's own childhood before such commonplace characters as the cane-wielding teacher and the slipper-whacking dad disappeared from British children's comics, for example.

Discipline and authority were upheld long after childhood, as such. With their children still living under their roof, it was perfectly normal for middle-class fathers to force, or at least *try* to force them to study what *they* wanted them to study—after all, who was paying for them to go to college? It was also perfectly normal for fathers to claim the right of veto—at the very least, of prior consultation—over their childrens' choice of marriage partners (Kafka's great love, Milena, was put away in an asylum for a whole year by her upper-middle-class dad for trying to marry a Jew). It was perfectly normal, too, to insist that your fine, highly educated, high-flying son merited a substantial dowry from the family of his bride-to-be (such demands were so normal among both Jews and gentiles before the Great War that professional dowry brokers were common—one called on the Kafka family on November 31, 1911).

Hermann Kafka insisted on none of these things. For all Kafka's complaining diary entries, Hermann seems to have been incapable even of browbeating his son to go with any regularity to the asbestos factory he had been eager to set up.

It's clear that an alternative picture of Kafka's father needs to be constructed: A man who had no idea of his son's nocturnal activities or sexual experience. A man who may have shouted and threatened in colorful images but who hardly if ever actually hit his son. A man who let his son study whatever he wanted in college, let him live rent-free even while he was pulling in many times a working man's salary, let him come and go as he pleased (in his early twenties, Kafka's nights out could easily go on until dawn), and let him choose his own fiancée without consultation and without insisting on squeezing a dowry out of her parents. A man who (unlike Professor Schnitzler) actually let his son treat a bookcase in the family home as genuinely private property.

A father, in other words, who, by the standards of the time (which are the only fair standards to measure him by) was, if anything, unusually liberal.

And since everyone else in this era (including Adolf Hitler) was writing about bold, sensitive sons standing up to ghastly hypocritical fathers who ruled the roost unjustly, it seems as if we really must take the "Letter to His Father" with a very large pinch of salt, indeed.*

Now, there's a good old Nietzschean argument that artists are somehow beyond truth and falsehood, that, as Ackroyd says of Dickens:

> Immediately he seized upon an opinion or a belief it possessed absolute truth and reality in his own mind. Everything in the world, therefore, took on the shape of his own principles or obsessions; this has nothing to do with lying unless creation itself is lie.

The great (and, in his personal life, often deeply unpleasant) playwright Bertolt Brecht was once asked, by an adoring listener, "Herr Brecht, what a wonderful story you have just told us! Is it true?" to which the cigar-smoking dramatist replied, with sovereign scorn, "Of course not. If it were true, it would not have been a good story."

However, we can't have this cake and eat it. Either there are facts (meaning that the stories people tell about them can be true or false), or everything is just stories and interpretations (meaning that "true or false?" is a wasted question). But if everything is just

---

*An extraordinary pinch of salt came to light in 2004. One Frantisek Basik had sat down in 1940 to write a memoir, purely for himself and his family. Basik had been an apprentice in a certain fancy goods wholesale business in Prague between 1892 and 1895—and had no idea whatever that the son of the owner, his one-time playmate, was already famous in literary circles and would one day become a legend. Basik's picture of Hermann Kafka is of an unusually kindly and jocular employer (at a time when apprentices in general were treated much as described by Dickens) who, it seems, hired Basik largely out of concern that young Franz had too few friends and was having trouble with his Czech at school.

stories and interpretations, why bother with any form of biographical investigation at all?

So instead of treating Kafka as some artist-superman dwelling in realms beyond normal categories of truth and falsehood, let's just say he was a man with a vast imaginary world, highly effective psychological defense mechanisms, and wonderful descriptive powers. And he was quite capable of writing letters to an imaginary person *whom he needed to exist.*

Myth 7: Kafka Was Crippled by TB for Years

Now, surely, if a man is fatally ill and knows it, that's going to have a pretty damn massive effect on what he writes, isn't it?

Well, yes. *If.*

It's very hard for us to imagine the world of people's medical hopes and fears from the days before antibiotics. Kafka had two younger brothers who died in infancy—at almost five year old, he would have been quite old enough to remember them, and it's hard to read his frequent images of people simply *disappearing*, being *struck out* or *swept away*, without wondering if the early memory of those absent brothers is at play.

But children *did* die in those days, all the time. Death and pain, in general, were far more frequent and visible than today, and far less predictable. Diagnosis was slow and inaccurate, treatment often ineffectual. People could and did drop dead virtually overnight from sore throats, say, just as they had done in the days of Jane Austen. The agonies Felice Bauer must have gone through to have almost all her teeth filled are virtually inconceivable to a modern Western dental patient. Syphilis was still fatal and *inherited* syphilis was one of the unspeakable ghosts haunting the age (which is why Ibsen wrote about it in those terms).

Against this general background of pain and dying—not to

mention, amongs the hecatombs of the Great War—a very common disease (it continued to be endemic in such places as Dublin and Glasgow until well after the Second World War) with no moral component, which kills slowly and (until the very final stages) without incapacitation or overwhelming pain, was seen very differently from the way we would see it now.

Although TB accounted for about one in ten of all Western deaths in the early twentieth century, diagnosis did not mean one had to despair of one's life. The disease was particularly associated with cold, damp living places, poor diet, and general stress. Being rich gave a person more chance of avoiding these ills, and the majority of middle-class patients eventually recovered more or less completely (as did Milena, for example) simply by leaving the dank cities, going to high altitudes for the clean air, relaxing completely, and eating well.

The fact that Kafka did *not* die in 1918 despite contracting the Spanish flu that killed so many other people (including his thirty-year-old cousin Irma) is striking proof that if you could, as Kafka did, take long, paid holidays in pleasant and healthy places, being diagnosed with TB was by no means a certain death sentence, and certainly not an imminent one.

Kafka's doctor was surprised to diagnose TB in a prosperous man of thirty-four with no family history of lung trouble. Among the most likely causes of infection, Kafka's own health faddery stands high on the list. Fans, like Kafka, of unprocessed food should remember that the Black Death was perfectly *natural*, *untreated*, and *organic*—just like the TB bacillus, which likes unpasteurized milk the best of all. As did Kafka, who, vegetarian that he was, drank what Samuel Beckett calls "the cow-juice" as freshly and naturally as possible, as often as possible.

Kafka's work place (being an insurance institute) was, by its very nature, a center of actuarial objectivity. So his bosses' reaction to his TB is perhaps the best indicator of how seriously a diagnosis was taken at the time. The answer is: seriously enough to give a man a lot of time off sick (so long as he could produce new doctors' notes regularly), but not seriously enough to let him retire on a pension or to stop promoting him.

Kafka did not even undertake any systematic treatment until over three years after the diagnosis, and it seems that he genuinely thought of his TB as somehow a psychological thing until he was actually confronted by the sight of other serious TB patients with undeniable (and stomach-churning) physical symptoms in early 1920.

In early 1922—almost four and a half years after being diagnosed—he had what he called a "breakdown." However, his diary entries for the time make no mention of *physical* pain or even weakness. There is "fear at the future," but that was there well before the TB struck. His present torments were caused (he wrote) by endless self-observation, isolation (now he *really* had the peace and quiet he always longed for), the feeling that he was trapped between two different time zones, and the question. "What did you do with the gift of sex?" (He had just been to a brothel.) And even so, within days of this "breakdown," he had the strength to embark on his most ambitious project since 1914, *The Castle*. And there's no doubt he was physically equal to the task, for in terms of sheer word count, the manuscript he produced in only eight months' (oft-interrupted) work is quite enough for a complete novel.

So Kafka's TB cannot account in medical terms for his virtual silence as a writer in the four and a half years following "The Great Wall of China." He didn't spend those years incapacitated and he didn't spend them—at least, he clearly didn't generally *feel* he was spending them—under imminent sentence of death. In fact, Kafka seems to have spent this time trying to work out where, how, with whom, and about what he was going to write in the future. He was looking for a replacement for what he'd lost, for the place he had done virtually all his writing—his home (and, by the end of 1918, his home*land*, itself).

His very first new entry in the so-called Hunger Artist Notebook of 1921 talks about writing an autobiography—but not so that he could treat his life as finished. He feels "like a man whose house is insecure and wants to build a new, secure one next door, if possible out of materials from the old one."

It's surely no coincidence that when he did start to write again at the end of January 1922, the main result was *The Castle.* That story (largely written back at his parents' place in Prague, with Kafka still on sick leave, still not pensioned off) took the search for a new home and a new place in life as its central theme.

In short, it wasn't Kafka's illness that virtually stopped him writing from mid-1917 to early 1922, thus depriving us of who-knows-what masterpieces.

The moral is: if you want to understand a man's writing, neither staring at photographs of his face nor even at X-rays of his chest is going to help.

But what about studying his closest relationships with other human beings? With, for example, the two women who received world-famous reams of letters from him? Surely *that* will give us insight into this remarkable mind?

Well, yes, it will—but only if we are prepared to look at the evidence with an open mind.

V

KAFKA AND FELICE:

NOTHING TO DO WITH SEX

Start of the marriage announcements in the *Prague Daily News*,
June 15, 1913, the day before Kafka sent
off his proposal to Felice.

This is where we leave historical facts and move into the world of human relationships. In this realm, as anyone who has ever had a relationship with another human being will know, facts are not the case at all. As we'll see later, Kafka's breakthrough story, "The Judgment," is one of the clearest and most unnerving depictions of this fundamental truth about human living. So what follows is just an opinion about a relationship and it will be very easy (because true) to point that out. With such a vast amount of personal material to deal with, it'll also be easy to accuse me of selectivity here and this will also, of course, be true: you can't *not* be selective if you want to tell a story.

My opinion will seem offensive to many people. So for once, before going over the parapet, I'm going to call in a small barrage from two of the biggest guns in Kafka studies, because my view of Kafka's relationship with Felice really just takes up from where the undisputed top Kafka scholars of Germany and Britain have already got. Alt of Berlin says:

Confronting the real Felice was, Kafka subliminally knew, a doubly risky business. It would reveal that he basically didn't find her very attractive and destroy the carefully built-up illusion of love that could only be produced through the medium of letters.

And Robertson of Oxford:

Sexual attraction, or even pleasure in her company, seem hardly to have existed . . . His more than 500 letters to her betray an immense emotional neediness, a desire to know about her life that suggests a wish for control, and a strange lack of intimacy.[1]

No attraction. No pleasure in her company, even. The carefully built-up illusion of love. What on earth was Kafka doing, courting for years a girl he didn't even *want*?

That's the mystery before us.

The Readiness Is All

Kafka clearly experienced a crisis in the last years of his twenties. This crisis led to his near-despair as a man and to his break-through as a writer. There's no contradiction in this, of course. Artists are often at their most desperately fertile when their lives are falling apart around them, because this is the very time they most need to feel (as Kafka put it) "protected" within the virtual world of their work.

There's nothing very unusual about a person having a big crisis in the last years of his or her twenties. If you're over thirty, you'll know this is true. If you aren't, you'll find out. There's nothing very unusual about the *sort* of crisis Kafka had in his late twenties, either. Which is unsurprising, given that he was human, not some kind of demigod.

The lighting on the world can seem to change almost overnight when you are in your late twenties. Questions that never entered your head at twenty-seven suddenly loom everywhere when your next birthday is thirty. Is the job you slipped into after college really going to be *your career, forever?* Isn't the exciting, fulfilling life you always sort of half-assumed would be yours taking its time a bit to come knocking on your door? Is *that* call, *that* e-mail, *that* meeting really ever going to happen? How many of your friends have quite suddenly seemed to pair off as steady numbers? Doesn't it all, quite suddenly, feel a just a little bit, well, *fragile?* Did you find yourself in a bar the other week with people who were all five years younger than you? Can you wait *much* longer before taking the plunge and getting into the housing market? If you don't, what's going to become of you? But if you *do,* well, good-bye to any hope of being able to switch jobs when you feel like it, take a second year off, *find* yourself . . .

So here's nothing terribly complicated about Kafka's dilemma at this time. This doesn't mean that it's easy to solve. Jumping off a bridge is not at all *complicated*, just very *difficult*, and any decent screenwriter knows that the strongest dilemmas are the simple, old ones.

In late 1911, Kafka's simple but intractable dilemma is this: he knows with inescapable logic that his absolute devotion to writing means a bachelor life—but, as his diary entries for that period make clear, he is all too frighteningly aware of what this will mean in reality.[2]

Dr. Kafka's Fight to Stay in Club 18-25

Kafka has, until now (he is twenty-nine), lived his adult life as carefree bachelor. He is notably young looking and, moreover, knows it. Most people, he informs Felice early on, "put me between eighteen and twenty-five." And he likes young looks in girls, too. He later warns Felice he finds it deeply unattractive that his sister has let herself go and changed from a "young girl" to a "bloated" motherly figure, "more out of carelessness and ignorance than from lack of time." He writes to Grete Bloch that he pities all girls because they have to change from girls to women.

Kafka's obsession with still looking like a member of the eighteen-to-twenty-five age group as he turns thirty is years ahead of his time. Until the 1950s, most young men aped the gravitas, hats, and social position of older male role models (e.g., Bogart). But Kafka would be perfectly at home in modern London or New York, surrounded by other thirty- (or even forty-) something singles desperately trying to stay young *looking* by means of ferocious diets and daily exercise.

Why is Kafka so worried about staying young-looking? For exactly the same reason people today worry about it, of course. Kafka wants to *appear* young because this will allow him to keep *behaving* as if he is young.

In the world of late-night cafés, clubs, and bars, whether we are taking about 2008 or 1908, appearances are everything. You stand or fall, are accepted or rejected, score or go home alone simply on the snap, dimly lit judgments of people who only know of you what you succeed in projecting.

One of Kafka's early stories, "The Refusal," is a wonderfully merciless snapshot of the visually driven, fashion-conscious, big-city meat market that could come straight out of a modern play by Patrick Marber or Neil LaBute:

The Refusal

When I meet a good-looking girl and say, "Please, how about coming with me?" and she walks straight past me without a word, what she means is this:

"You're no lord with a high-flown name; you're no broad-shouldered American who holds himself like an Indian brave, with straight-talking, easy eyes, your skin stroked with the air of wide grassy plains and the rivers flowing through them; you've made no grand journeys to great lakes and across them, to places I couldn't even find on a map. So you tell me, why should a good-looking girl go with you?"

"Oh, you seem to forget that you're not cruising down the street in some big, burbling limo; I don't see you surrounded by men dressed tight and smooth, murmuring your praises as they follow you in a perfect half-circle; your breasts look cute all modestly tucked up out of sight, but your thighs and hips make up for that; you're wearing one of those taffeta dresses with pleated folds that we all adored last autumn and yet there you go, smiling away even with that mortal danger hung around you."

"You know what? We're both right. And to save ourselves from becoming inescapably aware of it, what do you say we'd better each of us go home alone?"

This singles nightlife is the vital prop and escape valve of Kafka's day life, which is otherwise spent at home with his parents and at work. So long as he's able to cruise all-night Prague as a handsome, innocent young fellow just hanging out with his crew of well-off, clever, arty friends, all is well. A man like that has no disreputable plans or plots to seduce girls—he can just let fun things "happen" *to* him when (and with whom) he feels like it, in the Café Corso, the Trocadero, and similar places, which exist to make sure things like that *do* happen.

But what when the gang breaks up and the gray hairs start to show? When the happy world of the easy young man out with his pals and the party girls starts to fade into the seamy reality of the lonely bachelor hiring a "girlfriend" to provide sex and company (which is very clearly what Josef K. in *The Trial* has come to, at the age of thirty)?*

Time's winged chariot runs down everything that lives, but its headlamps hurry most scarily near in the rearview mirrors of the single.

The simple passing of time makes sense of the apparently bizarre accusation that the father makes to George Bendemann at the climax of "The Judgment": "Yes, you were actually an innocent child—but more actually, you were a devilish person!" Kafka uses an impossible comparison ("actually"—"more actually") to stress the way the father's accusation seems to lie beyond all logic. And so it does, but that doesn't mean it's impossible to understand.

In fact, we all judge like this. If we get trapped at a bar or in a party with someone who *looks* forty but still *acts* like twenty-five, we hastily make our excuses and leave because they make us feel uncomfortable. That embarrassing, too-old single person has *done nothing wrong* to anyone. They just haven't changed—and that means that *everything they do* is wrong. Not *morally* wrong, but wrong in a way beyond good and evil. They are the same person doing the same things as their younger selves had done, whom everyone was glad to see fifteen years ago. All they did was *not change*.

Time shifts the goalposts of innocence and experience. If we don't move in sync with it, we are condemned without having done a thing wrong.

Kafka, by 1911, can feel that court in session.

---

*Thirty then was forty now. Poor nutrition, low-level epidemic disease and non-existent preventive healthcare meant that what to us are middle-aged troubles—Felice's awful teeth, Kafka's obsession with his constipation and sleep—kicked in a good decade earlier.

A Wild Attempt at Escape

He knows by late 1911 that it's high time to grow up or grow seedy. But at this time, in this place—as still for most people now in most places on earth—*growing up* for a man nearing thirty means only one thing: *marriage*. And that almost inevitably means: *kids*. And that means that your fantasies about giving up the day job and devoting yourself to your writing are going to stay just that—fantasies.

The wildness of Kafka's thrashing against these looming chains is unforgettably palpable in his diaries of late 1911 and 1912. His desperation pushed him right to the boundaries of social convention. The entry of November 7, 1911, makes it clear that he was so head-over-heels infatuated with a penniless actress from the Yiddish theater that he came within an inch of making a complete fool of himself over her. He imagines the scene that did not (quite) happen when he tagged along (yet again) to finally see the performers off from Prague:

> I, a young man everyone thinks is eighteen, go up, in front of the evening's guests at the Savoy Café, with a circle of waiters standing by, before all the actors gathered at the table, go up to a thirty-year-old woman whom hardly anyone else even thinks pretty, who has two children of ten and eight, whose husband is right there beside her, who is a model of thrift and decency, go up to this woman and declare that I am completely in love with her . . .

Kafka's impossible object of obsession is simultaneously a good Yiddishe Momma and an adorable actress (which means, of course, both whore—anyone can pay to *look*—and virgin—no one can *touch*). She clearly represents a wild fantasy of somehow

short-circuiting the *marriage vs. bachelordom* choice he knows is
looming.

A Teenage Girl and Swedish Boys

At the end of June 1912, in Leipzig, Kafka is introduced by Brod
to Kurt Wolff (and his then partner Ernst Rowohlt). They invite
him to submit a book for publication.

Reviews and stories in magazines are one thing, but this is going
to be an actual, paid, publicized *book* with a fashionable publisher—
a watershed in any writer's life, and one Kafka clearly feels—he's
known since the age of thirteen that a writer is all he wants to be.[3]
When he gets back to the Prague café scene in August, he proudly
records that he is now able to hold the great and envied Werfel's
gaze all evening.

Meanwhile, this career development seems to spark off unusual
and extreme behavior. Immediately after being invited to submit
his book, he goes to Weimar and flirts—"successfully," says Brod's
diary—with the teenage daughter of the custodian of Goethe's
house, who is called Margarethe (the same name as the girl seduced
by Goethe's Faust).* He must have been sailing pretty close to the
winds of social convention here. Thence he goes to the nudist
Jungborn Sanatorium, where the doctor warns him against getting
too much moonlight and tells him of "specific exercises" that can
increase the size of the sexual organs. Kafka (having overcome an
initial unwillingness to take off his swimming trunks) poses there
as a life-drawing model, breaks into a sweat when talking to a
naked young aristocrat, finds himself wanting to lick the smooth
limbs of two Swedish youths, and dreams of the naked male guests
suddenly dividing into two parties and starting a vast fight.

---

*For the possible psychological significance of this, see Part VII: Kafka and Goethe.

This evidence is quite rightly quoted by anyone who sees a homoerotic side to Kafka. How significant it really is, is another question. For us in the twenty-first century, it's almost impossible to historically imagine an exclusively male world without coming to false conclusions. To men of Kafka's day, the natural objects of friendship, admiration, and true emotional attachment are all male. As, force majeure, are the objects of schoolboyish fumblings. Women are mothers, sisters, wives—unless they are *that* sort of girl.

Homosexuality? The very fact that in all his letters and diaries the only real suggestions of this feeling come at this time of intense mental turmoil is the best proof that it was, for him, most unusual.

He's in a real hothouse of conflict. He's about to have his first book published at last (having been writing solidly for about ten years). But his best friend and bachelor companion is about to get hitched; the second of his sisters, likewise. Right at the moment of his breakthrough, just when he most needs peace and security to follow his own inner star, the safe world of his extended adolescence is falling apart around him. He knows that it will very soon start to become deeply inappropriate for him to be living at home.

It's in this state of mind, a looming fear of being the last bachelor in town fighting it out with budding writerly hopes, that he meets Felice Bauer on August 13—having come to Max's place (i.e., Max's parents' place, their happy bachelor haunt) to finally decide on the order of the stories for his book . . .

A Hard-Working Girl

Including that meeting and their final one in 1917, Kafka and Felice met only seventeen times in all. Although they spoke the same language, they lived in different empires and an eight-hour train journey apart (and the Great War made travel much more difficult after July 1914). Running a relationship between Prague and Berlin in 1913 was rather like keeping one going today between London and New York.*

A long-distance e-mail relationship is perhaps a good way for the modern reader to imagine the whole business. Bizarrely, the Web has made it easier for us to understand the erotic charge of a relationship conducted purely in words than it would have been for people thirty years ago. Being able to correspond easily and quickly with people who live an impractical distance away means that you can entertain and confess and be bold and whatever, knowing that since your soul pal is in another country or even continent, you simply *can't* just jump into the car and drive to see him or her for real right now. You are just going to *have* to wait and get to know each other this way first. *Technology* has allowed *geography* to reerect the enticing barriers that *morality* can no longer provide. The keyboard is restored to its rightful place at the heart of the ar-

---

*Berlin was the senior partner in a special relationship. It had a hard-boiled talk-back humor which Felice used to imitate as her party *shtick*. So in this fantasy-update we should imagine Felice the hard-working New Yorker and Kafka the rather arty Londoner.

mory of seduction. Written romance is back (until universal web-cams spell the final triumph of the body over the spirit and sound the death knell of European dentistry).

And who better to seduce in 1912, by keyboard or pen, than the "writer of the clearest and most beautiful prose anyone is writing in German today"?

The effect on hardworking (and secretly stressed) Felice must have been spectacular. No beauty, she was no longer a spring chicken, either. It's only within the last thirty years that doctors have stopped looking sideways at women who delay having their first child into their thirties. Kafka, himself, thought his third fiancée, Julie Wohryzeck, was safely *past* the ticking clock at twenty-nine. An unmarried woman without private means in her midtwenties in 1912 would already be nervously eyeing the spinsterly shelf, while Papa would be getting restive at the thought of the growing dowry he'd have to pay up to make sure that his no-longer-quite-young princess stayed within the charmed circle of the middle class.

In Felice's case, things were especially fragile, thanks to her father's long-term adultery, her sister's unmarried pregnancy, and her brother's fecklessness (which in 1913 crossed over the border to outright dishonesty)—all of which she kept secret from Kafka at first (and then later hinted at in vain).

Into the life of this girl whose family is just hanging on to middle-class respectability, there suddenly parachutes the best friend of her relative-by-marriage, Bank Director Brod's son, a tall, handsome fellow with a rock-solid senior civil-service job, a man who is also a businessman in his own right—director of an asbestos factory—and who yet manages to be a real published writer (as so many educated young men long to be) with some rather glamorous friends like the boy-wonder poet Werfel, whom *everyone* has heard of.

An Unshakeable Judgment

He doesn't decide right away to write to her. On August 14, he tells Brod that his final ordering of the stories for *Meditation* was "under the influence" of her, and he's "thinking a lot" about her on August 15—but it's not until a week after their meeting that he actually describes it again to himself. It's as if she's slowly rising up from his subconscious.

If she'd read what he wrote on August 20 about her having seemed "like a servant" with a "bony, blank face that carried its blankness openly," her "almost broken nose," and her "rather stiff, unattractive hair," she'd have been pretty mortified. But as we've seen, making a lists of bodily flaws seems to have been Kafka's knee-jerk reaction to the pull of a woman, and he certainly saw or felt *something* that struck him powerfully that night.

As soon as he looked at her more closely, as he sat down, he immediately had (or, at least, he recalls a week later having immediately had) "an unshakeable judgment. The way the . . ."

His diary entry for August 20 breaks off dead at this point, as if hauled back from crossing some unseen threshold. We never get a hint as to *what* this "unshakeable judgment" was.

This is the heart of our mystery.

Whatever that judgment was, it takes another month for him to decide to write to her. It's maybe significant that, over those four weeks, his bachelor uncle from Madrid visits (Kafka questions him about his "dissatisfaction" with life) and his second sister becomes officially engaged. By September 12, he's thought about sending Felice flowers via an acquaintance.

For whatever reason, after almost a month, he decides to write to Felice. And when he does so, the thing that is most striking is that Kafka appears utterly *normal*.

The Respectable Wooing of Miss Felice Bauer

Most Honored Miss,

In the very likely event that you no longer have the slightest recollection who I am, I shall introduce myself again: My name is Franz Kafka and I am the man whom you greeted for the first time at Herr Director Brod's home in Prague, who later on passed to you over the table, one by one, photographs of a Thalian journey* and who finally took, in the very hand with which he now taps these keys, the hand with which you strengthened your promise that you would, next year, wish to go with him on a journey to Palestine.

This first letter is typed on headed paper from work, reinforcing the impression of a regular professional man of business. This also allows him to entertainingly blame the very nature of typing (which was central to Felice's own work-life) for his having become "carried away" in talking of their future correspondence—and for having made himself sound "much more difficult than I am."

No sign here that, in just two days' time, Kafka is going to sit down all night and write that extraordinary breakthrough story, that "perfect birth, covered with dirt and slime," "The Judgment," in which a man tries to break away from his childhood home (and childlike psychological binds) by getting engaged to a girl with the initials FB but fails because all his clever *writing* is no replacement for personal conviction.[†]

---

*Kafka means his and Brod's holiday to Weimar—"Thalian" because they went to see sights of poetic significance (Thalia is the muse of poetry and music). By showing that he assumes she'll get his high-culture code, Kafka subtly ticks a box in a very traditional opening letter from one educated and respectable person to another.

[†]Which, of course, exactly parallels the later failure of his letter-relationship with Felice. This is another example of Alt's theory as to why Kafka's works seem somehow uncannily to predict his life (i.e. because Kafka *the writer* sees more honestly than Kafka *the man*.)

Little knowing this, Felice seems to have replied in a friendly manner (we don't have her letters because Kafka destroyed them), allowing him to write his second to her on September 28. Here, Kafka still holds the disguise of the traditional wooer carefully in place. True, he admits that he is filled with indecision—but this state of mind, and his neuroses about the act of writing, are carefully presented in thoroughly conventional images. They are simply the (almost requisitely) turmoiled feelings of a would-be lover who, having bumped into the girl of his dreams, doesn't know whether he's coming or going or whether he dares write his love letter.

What moods take hold of me, miss! A rain shower of nervousness falls incessantly upon me. I want something one minute, I don't want it the next. When I'm up there on the stairs [at work], I still have no idea what state of mind I'll be in when I walk into the apartment. I have to pile up insecurities inside me before they can turn into a little security or a letter. How often!—so as not to exaggerate I'll say, for ten evenings—did I lie there before sleeping, composing that first letter in my head.[. . .] But at this rate I'll never come to an end. I'm chattering on about my last letter, rather than writing all the many things that I have now to write to you. Please understand the source of the importance that that letter of mine has gained for me. This has come about because you answered it, with the letter that lies here beside me, which gives me ridiculous pleasure and upon which I now lay my hand, so as to feel it in my possession.

He goes on to request a "little diary" giving him all sorts of details of her daily life. He ends by reminding her of his writing (he reports that his book has been "happily accepted" for publication)—but treats his art in a thoroughly brisk and businesslike way: "It's not very good, though. Better things must be written. And with this word of truth, farewell!"

By the standards of the day, this letter openly attempts to initiate a formal "correspondence" of the sort that would be generally considered as the first step on the path to the altar. Felice clearly knows that a boundary is being crossed, for she does *not* reply. No decent girl would, to such a clear invitation made so quickly.

Meanwhile, on October 7, Kafka's life hits a new crisis point. For the first time, his devoted and beloved youngest sister, Ottla (the only little sister still at home) sides with his father against him (thus completing the emotional constellation of *The Metamorphosis*). Even *she* can't understand why he refuses point-blank to take some kind of responsibility for the asbestos factory, which he was all for getting the family into and which could now plunge them into financial trouble. Kafka panics and writes to Brod that he can think of only suicide as the way out, relying as ever on Brod to sort things out.* Brod writes to Frau Kafka and she covers for her son's nonvisits to the factory while keeping Hermann in the dark.

The pressure that's been building is now hiked up even further. His first book is ready, he is certain (and rightly so) that his brand-new story is a massive breakthrough—but his secure old home life is in a state of total dissolution. Only frantic and undignified plots between Brod (who'll soon be married) and his mother can keep his childlike status intact. The desperate need to change his life utterly is clear.

By October 13, he can't wait any longer.

Fifteen days ago at ten in morning I got your first letter and a few minutes later I was already sitting down and writing four vast sides of paper to you. [. . .] Why have you not written back to me?—It's possible and, in that kind of writing probable, that there was some

---

*Stach suspects a bit of pretty hard emotional power-play here: "Kafka must have known what a heart-pounding calamity he was subjecting his friend and impresario to, having allowed Brod just two days earlier a look at his new writing."

kind of stupidity in my letter that could confuse you, but it is not possible that you could have mistaken the good intentions on which every word was based.

Still no reply. Kafka writes two more intense letters that he does *not* send off. Instead, he goes about things the regular middle-class way, by enlisting the very respectable support of Max's sister (married to Felice's cousin) to press his case. To her (knowing that it will get to Felice) he stresses that his long letter of September 28 may have been clumsy but was thoroughly "honorable."

"Good intentions" and "honorable" are, in 1912 (in German, as in English), code words laden with significance, when used of one's relationship with a respectable woman. They are clearly understood as steps in a marriage campaign—as is the use of relatives as intermediaries to press one's case. And what ardent lover is not occasionally "stupid or clumsy" in his eagerness to court his beloved?

Felice replies at last, on October 23, enclosing some pressed flowers (and the soothing claim that she *had* written to him but that the letter must have gone lost). Kafka's rejoicing is thoroughly in keeping with the conventional response of an Edwardian suitor whose advances have not, after all, fallen on stony ground:

Merciful Miss!

Even if all three of my directors were to crowd about my desk and look right down my pen, I must answer you directly, for your letter has come down to me as if from clouds to which one has been vainly staring upward for three weeks.

The next day, he writes to Brod's sister to thank her for her help. "Everything now seems to be in order," declares Kafka, quite the satisfied Kaiser-era wooer whose suit has been, in principle, allowed.

He now writes to Felice that "The Judgment" is coming out and will be dedicated to her, not because there's any real connection with her (which isn't what he'll say later to his diary) but simply because the story is, like him, trying "to be worthy of you from afar." The lost letter is mourned in a distinctly high-flown piece of suitor-speak: "So many years have passed without my hearing anything from you, and now another month of forgetfulness is thrown my way in such an unnecessary way."*

Forget for one moment *who* we are talking about and look at *what* we have in front of us. A prospective bride selected at a house party from one's own tight social/religious milieu, a respectable cultural excuse for opening the correspondence, helpers from the extended family enlisted, good and honorable intentions assured in writing, stupidity and clumsiness apologized for, heartache suitably experienced and relieved, dried flowers carried around in wallet together with letters from beloved, a story dedicated to her, sentiments gushingly expressed.

This is, quite simply, a good old-fashioned Victorian wooing. And to top it all, Kafka shows on October 27 that he has (as every good lover should) an almost photographic recall of everything that happened and was said on the night he met his instant beloved. By October 31, he is asking outright if he might be allowed to kiss her virtual hand.

By the standards of the day, there is no doubt at all what is going on here. This, remember, is still the world of Henry James as well as of Franz Kafka. Telling a decent girl in writing that you have honorable intentions, then asking for permission to kiss her hand is no laughing matter. A merely implied *understanding*

---

*It's pretty obvious that Kafka does not actually believe in it the lost letter at all. He conspires for now in the happy lie but again and again in the future he'll hint darkly about letters allegedly going missing.

between respectable persons (especially potent if, as here, her relatives have been deliberately involved) carries powerful social—potentially even legal—weight.*

Small wonder, then, that by the start of November, Miss Felice Bauer feels it proper to ask detailed questions about Dr. Franz Kafka's lifestyle . . .

Second Thoughts Unsent

Having established himself in those vital first impressions as a perfectly normal, if perhaps surprisingly urgent suitor, Kafka (now addressing her for the first time as "dear Miss Felice") reveals that writing is in fact all-important to him and that his entire life is arranged around it. He sets out the division of his days in extraordinary detail.

Clearly, Felice is surprised. She advises "goal orientation and moderation." He replies briskly that she wouldn't say this if she understood him properly.

Kafka reaches for his dog-eared Victorian Lovers' Phrasebook one last time, theatrically addressing his own heart when she agrees to write every day ("Hear, heart, a letter every day!"), but now that she's accepted his suit, the reality of what he's doing hits him. On November 9, he writes a letter ending it all, clearly saying that his devotion to writing can only make her miserable. He offers to return her letters and asks her to forget "the ghost that I am."

Writes—but doesn't *send*. Brod only found this letter after Kafka's death.

This is a vital watershed in the relationship. Kafka knows that

---

*As late as 1962, an Austrian woman successfully sued a man for engagement expenses (including a fur coat and a very large drinks bill for her friends) even though he claimed they had never been engaged and it had all been a joke. In the UK, Breach of Promise to Marry was not formally abolished until 1970.

he's going to make her miserable. But now the gloss of conventional half-truths gives way to outright evasion: the gap (which we know so well from the history of his fictional texts) between *what Kafka writes* and *what Kafka allows to be read* opens up in his personal life, as well.

Certainly, Kafka will tell Felice again and again, later on, that it can't work between them—yet he will never say it as plainly and honestly as in this unsent letter. He will always leave the door temptingly ajar.

With Love from Me to Thee

Instead of the outright and honest (and unsent) letter of November 9, Kafka sends one two days later in which he does indeed tell Felice they should end it. But in this letter he also says that he's setting her "the hardest test that anyone can set for the best-hearted of people"—then he totally undermines any sense of seriously ending things by using the familiar "thou" form for the first time.

Even today, the change of form from "you" to "thou" is an important social factor in Germany. Anglo-Saxons always find this business hard to navigate. Certainly, in 1912, it represented a formal and irrevocable change in the intimacy level of any German-speaking relationship.*

So, henceforth forever calling her "thou" in German (I'll stick with "you" in English to avoid our having to sound like some Shakespearian parody every time a letter's quoted) Kafka asks on November 11 why, since he belongs totally to her, he doesn't just "shut my eyes, throw myself into the train, and only open them again when I'm with you." The reason he gives is *not* that he is too

---

*For example, Kafka makes a particular note in his diary on the day he invites Felix Weltsch to use the "thou" form henceforth (23rd May 1912).

devoted to his writing. Instead, he reaches for the first time for the smokescreen that he is too *physically unhealthy* "for marriage and certainly for fatherhood." But he then undercuts this, too, by saying that when he reads her letter he feels he can *even overlook* his problem.

Sorry? *Overlook* a physical obstacle to marriage? What on earth does Kafka mean? Surely it's either a medical condition or it's not!

What Kafka's doing here is using for the first time one of his most potent and confusing tactics for avoiding giving Felice a straight answer: he's blurring the line between physiological and psychological barriers to their happiness. He also muddies things further by following up his first *we-must-end-it-all* letter by sending roses to Berlin ("Pathetic attempt, to send guiltless roses to follow such criminal words!" reads the accompanying note).

What on earth is poor Felice to make of this? Is her handsome and urgent suitor trying to hint at some actual disability or sickness he dare not name? Or is he just trying to plead in code for some especial female tenderness, love, and care? Understandably confused, she turns to her relative by marriage, Max Brod, for help. He writes to her that Kafka is the way he is because he refuses ever to compromise, that Kafka is special and needs to be treated with "understanding and goodness" and that he "is writing a novel that overshadows all the literature I know of."

The appeal to a traditional feminine role (plus the assurance that Kafka's writing will pay off) works. On November 14, she writes back to her suitor, also using the "thou" form for the first time. Kafka seems to go mad with relief. Her letter has made him utterly calm and

> it can only have been that "thou" that held me so, this "thou" for which I thank you on my knees, for it was the uncertainty about you that made me use it and now you send it back to me. You dearest person! Can I be certain of you now?

This "certainty" is clearly what Kafka needs: within four days (now addressing her as "my dearest") he's started *The Metamorphosis,* that amazing story which, whatever else it's about, is very clearly about a man who no longer belongs in his family's home but has nowhere else to go, even in his dreams.

Felice Gets Real

The steps of the dance that will go on for the following years are now fully set up. Quite understandably, Felice doesn't catch the unique doublethink going on in Kafka's head. It sounds as if he wants her, and indeed he does, but when he says (as he does again and again) that he wants to be "certain" of her, he means he wants to be certain that she's there to *write to* and report on his work to. He only wants her for one thing, and it's not sex.

When he reports on January 26, 1913, that he's been "utterly defeated" by the novel he's trying to write (*Amerika*) and will have to leave it for while lest "the cause" (*die Sache*) suffer even more, he goes on to talk about "a curious discovery" during the autopsy of Napoleon (i.e., the British doctor's claim that Napoleon was very poorly sexually endowed). He argues that there's no contradiction between Napoleon's famously evasive bedroom behavior to Josephine and his "letters clamoring about love." The parallel is pretty blatant: Kafka suggests that writing is *his* battlefield, the place where *his* "cause" will be won or lost, that a man may pen glowing love letters while avoiding the marital bed—and that Napoleon's womenfolk were devoted to him for something other than sex.*

---

*It seems unlikely that Kafka really did suffer from this physical lack (or even seriously *feel* that he did), for there's no mention of it before Felice or after her. The prospect of sex with someone you don't actually fancy has inevitable consequences and Kafka's alleged Napoleon Syndrome is surely just the equivalent of a sudden headache or feigned inebriation.

He already has what he needs—a virtual lover to make possible his impossible fantasy of escaping lonely bachelordom yet still being free. He just wants the "quiet, beloved presence" (*presence?* She's in Berlin) that helps him to write (March 28, 1913). He desperately puts off another meeting. But this isn't Second Life. Felice is, inconveniently, a genuine person only eight hours away by rail, and to keep her "presence" he's obliged to keep up the fiction that he really wants *her*, the flesh-and-blood woman.

A meeting cannot be put off forever, and when it happens, the incongruity of the real world and Kafka's imaginary world is becoming apparent. Their actual encounter for a single afternoon on March 23 is so unsuccessful that neither of them wanted to try it again over the weekend Kafka planned to spend in Berlin. Instead, in May he meets up with other Wolff & Co. authors in a Berlin café, where they write a joint card to their beloved publisher. Even then, in the better world of his head and letters Felice is still "my only goal on earth" (May 13).

On May 23, 1913, the worlds collide at last. Kafka reports that he has *still* not written to her father asking for her hand, because he first needs a medical opinion on the mysterious problem that could mean they can't marry (he continues to mix psychology and physiology, for he doesn't exclude the possible "miracle" that being with her might "cure" him). He suggests that he ask her father to recommend a doctor.

Felice can stand any amount of mind games—but she won't take his going against the social formalities that are her ultimate guarantee. She uses the one power she has over him and stops writing back.

Letter-less, his virtual world crashes. "For God's sake, why don't you write to me? No word for a week. That's truly horrible" (May 25, 1913). He says it's all over, clearly implying that it's all her fault: "By your silence, you end my hope of the only happiness that is possible for me on this earth." But instead of walking away, he puts a killer drop shot back into her court by saying that he'll "belong" to her as soon as he hears *"the softest call, so long as it's genuine"* (May 27, 1913—Kafka's stress).

She gives in and writes again. But she fought back and Kafka now knows he can't keep stalling. The reality of life, the life where promises actually *mean* something and involve *people,* is knocking at his study door. If he wants Felice, he's going to have to *have* Felice.

Kafka's strategy now changes and the unedifying game moves on to the next stage, with his proposal of marriage on June 16, 1913.*

A Prenuptial, 1913 Style

The proposal, itself, is hardly ecstatic. Having once again stressed that he needs a doctor's opinion before writing to her parents (adding for good measure that a doctor's opinion will not necessarily be decisive for him anyway), Kafka goes on:

> But there's no time for longer delays, at least I feel it that way, and that is why I ask: will you, under the above conditions, which are sadly not to be avoided, consider whether you want to become my wife? Do you want that?

There follows a many-page barrage of riders, some of which are blatant invention. "I have no memory, either for things I've learned

---

*A look at the *Prague Daily New's* marriage-advertisements for June 15, 1913, the day before Kafka completed and sent off his proposal, gives a priceless snapshot of for that year. Five marriage brokers offer their services. Seven of the forty-six adverts, like private car-for-sale ads today, state roundly "no canvassers" (*keine Vermittler*). Twenty put an actual figure on the dowry offered or demanded. A Doctor of Law (like Kafka), aged 33 (Kafka is not quite 30 yet) and (like Kafka) in the civil service, but only in a "large German provincial town in Northern Bohemia," feels able to demand a dowry of "not less than 100,000 crowns" (say, $1.5 million at today's values). It seems realistic rather than merely cynical to wonder whether this helps explain why Felice and her family put up with so much.

or read, for things I've experienced or heard, for people, or events," claims Kafka—this being the same man who last year had an almost total recall of their first meeting more than two months after it happened. He throws back her humble readiness to be guided onward and upward (she seems to have written that he's "further on" than she is). What is needed in marriage is not equality at all, says Kafka—but people who simply feel that they "necessarily belong together" and who therefore do not "disturb the freedom of each individual in the slightest."*

The next day, he demands a "point by point" rebuttal of all his arguments against marriage—then adds (in a way that must have totally wrong-footed Felice) that he wants her to send over a Berlin newspaper because he's heard there's a review of "The Stoker" in it.†

Despite all this, Felice doesn't have to think long about accepting his proposal. She seems to have replied in the affirmative more or less by return post. But if she imagines that a speedy, loud, and clear yes is what Kafka needs to set his poor mind at ease from the oft-mentioned "torture of uncertainty" (May 18), she has another think (and many dismaying letters) coming.

For a start, Kafka doesn't accept her acceptance as a real yes at all. "I am holding my hand over your mouth and for now you haven't really said that word, you've merely spoken into my hollow palm" because "I do not see that you've answered everything point by point" (June 20).

Kafka's letters in this period make deeply unattractive reading, and it's just no good for his adoring biographers to suggest that it's all merely the coruscating honesty of a man who cannot

---

*Kafka here sounds remarkably like Hegel fudging the issue between (Prussian) State power and Individual Freedom—a fudge that bedevilled German thought and ultimately brought out the devil in it: if people "necessarily belong together" (which they know by their *feelings*, not by reason) they don't need to worry about "the freedom of the individual."

†It's that roaring good review by a man whose own work came out earlier this year in the same volume as *The Judgment*.

bear, as a less scrupulous man would, to hide his faults from his bride-to-be.

In the summer of 1913, Franz Kafka isn't courting any more: he's negotiating.

Marriage, in 1913, was for the duration. It remained so for many decades. Divorce was a rare, difficult, and costly form of social near-suicide until the sixties. Right up until the new social era witnessed by such TV shows as *Friends*, vast numbers of sitcoms, dramas, and murder tales depended completely on the underlying assumption that marriage is essentially unbreakable. The last great example is the immortal *Fawlty Towers*. In these scenarios, the characters can't escape *from* the marriage, so they score points off each other to see who'll dominate *within* it (or even plot to kill each other to escape it).

Kafka's correspondence with Felice after she gives her yes must be seen in this light. It is *not* some invitation for her to back off and away. On the contrary. The letters of late June, July, and August 1913 are a bizarre and ruthless campaign to get an ever more exact, clause-by-clause "yes"—to extract a sort of prenuptial agreement (*in writing*, of course)—from Felice.

But what *is* it that he wants her to agree to? The short answer, is: everything. Kafka wants a totally blank marital check and, with Felice's yes in his pocket, he pushes things ever further.

He's already been through his supposed medical problems. He now adds the bare-faced lie that his job is not at all secure and that his superiors have their eye on him for his failures (June 22). He says they'll be poor (his income in 1913 is 4½ times that of the average workers in the factories he inspects). He claims—nothing in his life suggests this is true—that he wants to live in the (non-Jewish German) suburbs of Prague. He warns her she'll be "horribly alone" there—could she bear it? "I must have a completely exact answer to this, Felice, surely you can see that, a completely exact answer" (June 21).

He makes sure she knows how he hates playing with children. He stresses how he despises his sister for having let her body change from that of a "young girl" into a "bloated" mother figure. He demands that she ignore anything Max or anyone else says: "You must only listen to what I now write, Felice, you must only answer that, but you must answer everything, and not just the questions" (June 23).

Just saying yes again and again to marriage is not enough—Felice must give an exact, precise and *written* yes to every detail of the married life to come. She must be left *nothing* that she could ever hold against him once the banns are read.

It's a game she can't win. When she claims to be fine about a specific problem (such as the alleged poverty they face), he says this doesn't count because she must simply not have thought it through properly (June 26). It becomes clear that what Kafka demands from Felice is the Luther-style declaration of unconditional conviction that he'll often hint at in his writings. He wants a yes that will go beyond all logic. He needs her to say, "'I can do nothing else, despite everything.' But by all appearances, you can't and mayn't say that" (June 27).

She still takes it—so he still pushes, now into darker regions. On July 6, he informs her that he's been to "a cabaret that my wife wouldn't be allowed to go to" and that he "generally has very much of a feel for such things," although without her there he "almost completely failed" apart from when watching "a dancing and singing Negress." The next day, he doubts whether he is human at all, and the day after, tells her, "You do not know, Felice, what literature is in some heads." He asks her to "consider the things I haven't said, as well!" (July 10) and warns, "There are still some horrible corners in me that you don't know."

Is he hinting at his old nightlife and his locked bookcase? We'll never know, because he never says exactly what he means. But his hammerings at Felice suggest a prospective bridegroom attempting to extract an indulgence for *whatever* he wants to do after they are married.

Still, Felice doesn't run. Then, on July 13, Kafka suggests that he *not* write to her parents after all but that the couple "stay as we are" at least until Christmas. It's May 23 all over again: She'll put up with all his demands—but not with his putting things off. She invokes her only defense and stops writing again.

And it works again: Kafka mutates instantly back into the baffled, suffering lover: "I can't understand what's happened. My letter must have hurt you, there's no other possibility. But if it hurt you, you must have misunderstood it . . . Felice, please, write a word to me, be it good or bad, don't make my wretchedness greater than it is" (July 19). She keeps up the dreaded silence and, by July 28, he is begging: "No letter again. How you torture me like this, Felice!"

Strange Travel Plans and Mysterious Promises

Felice gives in yet again. And no sooner has she relented than Kafka has an idea "which, if you like it, would be great" (August 2).

He's refused to join her family's holiday for a few days on the North Sea island of Sylt, claiming work demands, but now he says (staying carefully in the conditional) that he could write to her father, meaning that "we'd be formally engaged in our parent's eyes in maybe fourteen days." It's clear that his tempting plan is conditional on his "new idea—here it comes."

Kafka's great new idea is that rather than *his* going to Sylt, *she* should come "for few hours" to Prague "on the way back to Berlin."

Prague? *On the way back to Berlin* from the North Sea? A quick look at the map of Europe suggests that Kafka either had a profound ignorance of geography or a profound grasp of emotional game playing. He's suggesting it would be a great idea for her to

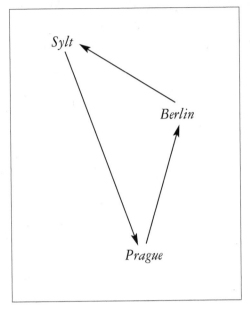

Kafka's plan for how Felice could call in for
a few hours "on the way home."

spend two entire days on trains so that she can see him for a few hours.

The next day, while his great new idea is still en route to Sylt, Kafka follows it with a rather curious request. He wants Felice to promise "with solemn words" to do something "without question and completely"—without telling her what. He assures her that it's nothing impossible or bad, but won't say any more. He also tells her that he can hardly see himself coming to visit her in Berlin a single time, even if they don't get married until next May.

Absurd itineraries, secret promises, veiled threats: what on earth is Kafka up to? Well, we should remember that he's just accused her of "torturing" him gratuitously by her long silence. When you look at the letters and not the myth, it's very hard to see anything else here than a set of power games in which Kafka is reasserting control. He repeats his travel plan enthusiastically (complete with the killer phrase "on the way back") on August 4.

By the sixth, he has the only answer anyone could reasonably have expected. But now he's able to act as if *he's* the injured party and *she's* the one making excuses to put off a meeting that "would have been the simplest thing in the world. And so lovely, too." He immediately turns the screw by telling her that "it's now absolutely necessary" (he doesn't say why) for him to spend his whole month's holiday in a sanatorium.

The following day, he reveals what he has made Felice promise to do. He wants to control her body. She has unknowingly vowed to follow his beloved Müller exercise system (a ladies' version of which has just come out) "slowly, systematically, carefully, thoroughly, daily." In the same letter, he says that he assumes their household will be vegetarian.

Five days later, he quotes back at her, verbatim, several lines of the letter he got on August 6 (the one that quite rightly called his travel plans "stupid"). He says it's "necessary" to do so. By refusing to take a detour halfway around Europe to visit him, she's undermined all the "security" he got from her. Which makes it *her* fault that they now won't meet until Christmas, at the the earliest.

See how useful written documents can be (especially in the hands of a trained lawyer)?

On August 12, he writes to her that he doesn't feel her "convinced decisiveness" anymore and, the next day, takes up his diary again (after a gap of three weeks) to note that it may now all be over between them.

Kafka's diary for August 14 read in tandem with his letter to Felice of the same day feels almost psychotic—and raises fundamental questions about the diary itself as record of facts. In his diary, Kafka says he loves her and "couldn't withstand" her letters. He then goes on to write one of his most famously gloomy descriptions of sex: "coitus as the punishment for the pleasure of being together." This is usually quoted (like so much of Kafka) out of context. It's, in fact, not some global comment on sex at all—it's clearly about the specific prospect of married sex with Felice.* But that very day, he writes to her parents at last—and then fires off a letter to Felice that almost takes one's breath away.

He's obviously furious that she's has asked a graphologist to look at his handwriting. Someone he doesn't even know has been invited to peer into the locked bookcase of his psyche via that most personal thing, his writing itself. How dare the man say that he is "highly sensual"! He has, he'll have her know, "enormous inborn capacities for asceticism." He is supposed to have "artistic interests"? *Interests* indeed—he "consists of literature and am nothing else." Kafka, his German now sounding almost like an official letter, ends with a extraordinarily implied threat to his betrothed and a blatant laying-down of the law:

> I follow your graphologist with a critic. In the *Literary Echo* there recently appeared a review of *Contemplation*. It's very charming, but otherwise unremarkable in itself. There is only one notable section: in the course of the review, it mentions "Kafka's bachelor art . . ." What do you say to that, Felice?
>
> To deal with the other points swiftly: I absolutely insist on the Müllerizing; the book will go out to you today; if you find it boring that's because you aren't doing it properly; exert yourself to do it quite exactly (*in very careful stages, naturally!*) and the immediately tangible effect will mean you won't be able to find it boring; don't worry yourself about the [vegetarian] cooking; as for your sleep-talking cousin; when she's asleep, carefully lay a cloth over her face.
>
> Franz[†]

---

*Coitus as punishment for being with someone you don't actually find attractive.

[†]It's notable that Kafka 'absolutely insists' Felice should exercise the very day after deciding sex with her would be a punishment.

He's putting his foot down all right—no wonder he writes in his diary the next day that

> my ever-increasing inner decisiveness and conviction contain possibilities that may let me fight my corner in a marriage and even guide it so that it will be a development advantageous to my calling.

His marriage "a development advantageous to my calling"? Yes, it would seem that what Graham Greene called the writerly "chip of ice in the heart" is well and truly there. Even the ever-protective Brod, father of the entire K.-myth, was obliged to confess that Kafka's campaign to marry Felice was "a life plan without any individual significance, independent of the bride as a person."

Bit tough on the girl in question, that.

Long Live King Kafka!

Dr. Franz Kafka wants a life dedicated to writing. Fair enough. But he also wants one in which someone will be there when he wants her to be—the way Ottla was there for him when he walked straight into her room at dawn, having just been up all night writing "The Judgment."

His post-yes campaign is an attempt to get Felice to agree, absolutely and as a matter of record, to a marriage in which his writing—not love, not sex, not children, not comfort, just his writing—will be the center of everything. And to get her to do so *without his even asking for it outright.*

As he'll put it later, discussing her part in the "guilt" of their failed relationship, he never suggested what he would have really liked, but if *she'd* only suggested this he would "not have known what to do for happiness."[4]

What's strange is that it is 1913. If all Kafka wants is a marriage where the man gets what he wants, especially if his work is involved, no questions asked, well—that's simply what marriages usually *are* in 1913 (and for long afterward). So if millions of other men have obedient wives, why can't Kafka ask for it straight out?

Kafka, like so many of his heroes, is trapped in a deadly halfway house between tradition and modernity. He doesn't *want* to be like millions of other traditional men—and most important, he doesn't want to be like *one particular* traditional man.

Like many educated, sensitive sons of self-made, uneducated men, Kafka views his father as the last thing on earth he consciously wants to be. His entire self-image is that of a writer, an artist, a seeker after pure modern truth—the absolute 180° opposite of his shop-keeping, money-grubbing, hypocritical Victorian father. How can he admit, even to himself (*especially* to himself) that he is fatally drawn to what is essentially just a re-creation of what his blustering, coarse, bad-mannered father has got?

Because this is what it all adds up to. In Kafka's wish-marriage, it is *he* who insists that *his* food fads, *his* taste in furniture, *his* body clock, *his* (non-) sexual moods, *his* social life (if he wants one at all), *his* Müllerizing (which his wife will dutifully have to follow), *his* desire to go out for a walk alone if he feels the need, will be the laws around which the new household revolves. And how will he justify all this? Why, just like his father does—by appealing to *his work*, of course.

Can Kafka really not hear that, when writing to Felice's father about his "immutable destiny," he sounds extraordinarily like Thomas Mann's splendidly wretched writer claiming an "inescapable calling" in the little masterpiece *Tristan* (1903)? Apparently not, even though Kafka admired Mann deeply and had surely read this story.* Everyone has their blind spots, and when it

---

*Kafka says it's his "unabänderliche Bestimmung" to write, while at the comic high-point of *Tristan* Detlev Spinell appeals to his "unausweichlicher Beruf."

comes to defending his right to write, everything else—even his vaunted self-awareness—falls by the wayside.

Kafka's writing shall be the undisputed fulcrum of the new Kafka household, just as Hermann Kafka's business is the undisputed fulcrum of the old one. This is not a matter of *choice*, of course, simply the way things *must* be.*

Must it be? Yes, it must be! Down with Kafka the meat-eating, shop-keeping, card-playing ruler of the old Kafka household—long live Kafka the leaf-eating, book-writing, Müllerizing ruler of the new Kafka household!

And so the mystery reveals itself.

Now we see why Kafka reacted so excessively when Felice chose heavy, traditional furniture for their home-to-be. It wasn't some mere difference in taste that made him hear a death knell. Her choice almost gave his subconscious game away. He *had* to react wildly against it. His marital furniture *had* to be totally different from his parents' furniture. It had to look modern and radical—because otherwise the re-creation of Hermann Kafka's kingdom would have been all too cryingly obvious.†

The Unshakeable Judgment Revisited

Let's look again at what Kafka wrote after his first meeting with Felice. What he saw was a woman who

looked like a servant even though she was sat at the table. And I was not in the least curious about who she was, but immediately felt at ease with her. Bony, blank face that bore its blankness openly.

---

*In the summer of 1913, Kafka bangs endlessly on about "necessity," that favorite concept of every German since Hegel who ever planned to do something morally dubious.

†When he (not for the last time) harps on about *that* furniture after the bust-up, Kafka explains: "I haven't founded a business that's going to develop itself married year by married year, I don't need a home for good, to provide the ordered peace from which I shall guide this business." Which comes very close to saying out loud "I am *not* my father!".

Blank, "empty," it's the same word in German. This, you have to suspect, was the secret "unshakeable judgment" that Kafka felt that night. Here (he knew it deep in his psyche the moment he looked more closely at her) was the woman for him. A marriageable woman of his own class and religion, but one so nondescript you could almost mistake her for a servant. A woman he felt no desire at all to learn more about. A woman whose empty face was waiting to be written on like a blank sheet of paper . . .

This isn't the end of the story, of course. The worm turns with a vengeance later. Face-to-face, Kafka, the ringmaster of the written word, is no match for Felice's Prussian straight-talking. At the Berlin Zoo in March 1914, she turns his renewed proposal down and makes him back off from his position of un-alterable "necessity." He promises to try to change. As he will bitterly recall on April 4, he even falls so low as to bring up the asbestos factory in his attempt to show her how he could be a better husband!

Kafka thrashes about for help to regain control, writing to her parents (as does his mother).

Meanwhile he also arranges a fall-back position. On March 13, he makes detailed arrangements with Felice's best friend, the younger, prettier Grete Bloch, to meet up with him alone for a weekend sometime soon. He seems to think it a done deal on March 18. Four days later, he openly says that he thinks it's all over with Felice, in which case (says he) he'll soon be free. On the April 18, it's Grete, not Felice, who gets the impressive news that the classy *New Review* has not only accepted *The Metamorphosis* but also made him those "other charming offers." In mid-June, he tries blatantly to set up spurious "business reasons" for Grete to be sent to work in Prague.*

---

*It's been claimed—Max Brod believed it at least for a time—that Grete had a child by Kafka. Alt's mighty biography says firmly that this is impossible: Grete resisted Kafka's "innocent" invitations to meet up alone, knowing full well what would happen.

Grete, though, belatedly chooses loyalty to Felice. Kafka seems to see the disaster coming at the last minute. His letter to her of July 3, 1914, is an almost open plea not to betray him. But it's too late. Felice gets to see edited versions of the letters Kafka sent to Grete. Even with the most damning parts quite literally cut out (with scissors, by Grete), it's too much for her to take . . . at least, for the time being . . .

The story goes on until December 1917, but it would need an entire book to retell it. For us, now, looking at the K.-myth, the point's surely been made. Whatever suffering was caused in this famous relationship wasn't due to Kafka's excessive honesty or merciless self-analysis—and it wasn't caused *to* Kafka.

If Kafka's relationship with a woman he wanted to marry but didn't actually find at all attractive was (perhaps inevitably) somewhat fraught, what about his *other* famous relationship—with a woman he most certainly *did* want to bed?

Enter Milena.

VI

KAFKA AND MILENA:

ALL ABOUT SEX

Headline from the *Prague Daily News*, October 29, 1918, announcing the establishment of the new state of Czechoslovakia. Kafka thereby acquired the same nationality as Milena.

Writing Sex

Kafka often hints pretty strongly at bizarre, taboo-breaking sexuality in his published work—a father's dirty underwear, a woman with her hand deep inside her fur muff, a vision of a man-beetle kissing his sister's neck, a gaping wound in a man's thigh—but his published work never actually contains sex. "A Country Doctor" comes close, but even here the demonic servant's attack on the maid is more cannibalistic than sexual; in "A Report for an Academy," the primate hero has a half-tame female chimpanzee with whom, "I enjoy myself the way apes do," but that's as explicit as Kafka gets anywhere. Otherwise, his published characters—even in "Turned Down," that little a story about an attempted nightlife pickup, don't ever even *think* openly about sex.

His unpublished work is different. In *The Trial*, Josef K. puts off his weekly visit to his whore to lurk in wait for Fräulein Bürstner.

Her name can translate as "Miss Scrubber," her unrespectability and "uncleanliness" has already been mentioned by the landlady. K. thinks of her as "just a little typist who wasn't going to resist him for long" and ends up kissing her throat like a thirsty animal. Later, he openly wants to physically possess the "young woman" who cleans floors for the court. Leni, the lawyer's young "care," literally pulls Josef K. down to her onto the carpet. Frieda in *The Castle* rolls with K. in the puddles of beer and filth under her bar. It's notable that all of these scenes are scented with dirt and/or whoredom.

We might argue that this is because when Kafka was writing, no one published open sex scenes yet. No doubt this is true, but we have wonderful evidence that in the privacy of his own study, Kafka found it hard to write such material. He started *The Castle* writing as "I." This worked fine for Kafka throughout the world-famous opening scenes. The now-immortal "K." only appeared when he got to the sex scene with Frieda (which was originally somewhat stronger than the version we now know). It's as if Kafka quite literally *couldn't* write about a sexual encounter with himself in the picture.

As for his life, we already know all about the locked-away porn and brothels of his twenties, about sweet Hansi Szokoll and the Brünhilde of the Trocadero. In July 1920, Brod writes that to Kafka, the grand passion for Milena means "salvation from sex." In January 1922, Brod is "deeply dismayed" by Kafka's report of his last definitely known visit to a brothel (just days before he starts *The Castle*); he notes how Kafka is "tortured" by sex. And Kafka's diaries from those days confirm it: "Sex drives me, tortures me by day and night," he writes. He has always been ready for an "opportunity that offers itself quickly, near, and willingly"— but such things do not of course really happen of their own accord, and he admits that he has always known how to "bring about, to attract 'opportunities'" that are in fact "vile" things to be absolutely avoided (January 18, 1922).

So the question is: how on earth did his writings and his biographical facts (which are all perfectly well known) both give way to the myth of a Kafka who was otherwordly about sex?

Staring at Milena

The chief witness for the K.-myth, when it comes to sex, is Milena.

Everyone loves Milena. Kafka's adoring fans love her because (unlike Felice) she fits the young/sexy/creative/intense bill for a Great Artist's Lover. Some critics love her because she was an activist who died for her politics under the Nazis. Some love her because she was a Modern Woman. Some love her because she was a writer who translated Kafka into Czech and some love her because she shows how much Kafka loved Czech culture.

But everyone loves her one way or another and this has led to her statements on Kafka (her letters to Brod and the obituary she wrote for the press, all of which Brod published in his biographies) being taken absolutely at face value. She, via Brod, is the origin of our lasting image of Kafka as "a man so terrifyingly clear sighted, so pure, so incapable of compromise that he is compelled to live ascetically."[1]

There's no doubt that Kafka was head over heels in love with Milena, and one can see why.

She was young (twenty-three to his thirty-six), Czech, and sexy. In her teens she had hung out with Werfel's Prague café circle, dressing in bohemian clothes, experimenting with (stolen) drugs, deliberately flaunting her sexuality, ending up needing an abortion before she went to college. In this sense she was like the Czech

"sweet maidens" Kafka had always liked. But she was also throughly upper middle class and educated. She had been locked up in a mental home for nine months for disobeying her father's wishes in wanting to marry Ernst Pollak, a Jewish member of the arty Arco circle. Yet when Kafka met her, she was outwardly a respectable married woman—and a writer.

This all meant that she could be a girlish "little Milena" or an experienced "Mother Milena" to Kafka as the occasion demanded. A perfect mix, in other words, of virgin and mother— with a touch of the nightlife whore thrown unspokenly in to complete the classic sexual trinity (in Kafka's first recorded dream of her, she's in a café wearing grotesque amounts of face powder).

The final seal was that *she* came on to *him* by asking if she could translate his work into Czech. When we remember how writing was (it sometimes seems) almost literally a sexual experience for Kafka, Milena could have done nothing more guaranteed to attract him.[2]

As with Felice, Kafka takes some time to decide to write to Milena—no doubt partly because at the time he actually met her, he had recently become engaged to Julie Wohryzeck and Milena was already married. Once the letter writing starts, however, there is very little beating about the bush.

In his very first letter, Kafka implicitly suggests that she come to his sanatorium in Merano. In his second letter, he invites her openly. By June 1920 (just two months after their correspondence begins), he is offering to pay her rent if she moves out from her husband (just until she gets better, of course, and with no strings attached, naturally).*

Once again, Kafka has used the magic of writing to build a virtual world in which one brief meeting has blossomed into a full-blown affair. But this time, he really *does* want the woman. And briefly, he gets her. Kafka has four deliriously happy days with Milena in late June and early July 1920, after which he tells the hapless Julie about his (long-planned) infidelity.

The earth clearly moves for Kafka in the Vienna woods. Not that it is simple: in Milena's famous letter to Brod of January or February 1921, she said that "the uncovered flesh is too revealed, he can't stand the sight of it." When this problem arose, Kafka and Milena stared into each other's eyes "as if unable to breathe or as if our feet hurt" until the attack passed.

In mid-July 1920 Kafka is still on cloud nine, confidently expecting Milena to leave her husband and come to Prague: "Whatever happens, it will happen with you nearby" (July 14).

---

*Any more than there had been explicit strings when he offered to pay the rent for the Germania of the Trocadero a decade earlier. Back then, he had "laughed as though he was being ironic" while making the offer. Brod at the time found this "strangely reticent."

Kafka, Happy but Still Not Quite Straight

It's an extraordinary time in Kafka's life and no one can read his letters from it without being deeply moved. Here is man who is suffering from a quite probably fatal disease, living in a strange ghost world now that the Prague where he spent all his first thirty-four years has been blown away (along with his savings) by the war. Almost the only thing he's written in the last three years is a vast, unsent letter to his father. Having spent five years in an abortive double engagement, he's theoretically engaged again but has put off the marriage and come away alone. And now along comes this young, much-desired, vivacious, highly intelligent girl who wants to transform him into a *Czech* writer, a real citizen of his new country, and seems to be brilliant at it. And who loves him enough—not just in letters but in real life, in the real Vienna woods!—to put up with his troubled sexuality, too.

No wonder Max Brod has never seen Kafka so happy and never will again. Kafka's total candour to Milena is in doubt, even now, however. There's a wonderfully entertaining example of this in Peter-André Alt's splendid book.

On August 1, 1920 (when he's still confident that she will soon be his) Kafka, having made many excuses as to why he couldn't come to Vienna again, has a new plan—"how it didn't occur to me before"—which means they can meet up every weekend in the Czech-Austrian border town of Gmünd for a decent chunk of time without his having to take time off from work or her having to spend a suspicious night away from Vienna. Across three letters he sends detailed Prague–Vienna train timetables to Milena. It is surprising that this plan "didn't occur" to Kafka before, because it *did* occur to him before—in March 1913, to be precise, when he sent *exactly the same timetable* to Grete Bloch, trying to arrange a weekend rendezvous in Gmünd with her, behind Felice's back.

Milena, of course, didn't know that she wasn't the first girl to have been offered this handy tryst-by-timetable. In fact, you suspect that she really knew very little about Kafka.

> Life for him is a thing completely unlike life for everyone else, above all money, the stock market, the foreign exchange, the typewriter are all completely mystical things (which they indeed are, it's only we who do not see it), they are strange puzzles to him . . . he doesn't understand the simplest things . . . this whole world is and remains a puzzle to him. A mystical secret. Something he can't manage and which he admires, with touching naivety, because it is "businesslike." When I told him about my husband, who is unfaithful to me a hundred times a year, who holds me and many other women under a sort of spell, his face lit with the same respect as it did when he spoke of his boss, who can type so quickly and is therefore such a fine man . . . He is completely incapable of lying . . . [3]

This is the same man who held down a high-flying legal job efficiently for years.* The same man who eagerly anticipated how much interest he'd get from his war bonds. The Kafka who owned pornography, appeared in court, hid money from his family, went to brothels all his adult life, kept a complete set of his reviews, paid the rent for an amateur prostitute, cheated in mind (more than once) on his first fiancée and did so in deed (with Milena, herself, who seems to conveniently forget this fact) on his second.

---

*And who, in December 1912 took a break from writing *The Metamorphosis* and *The Man Who Disappeared* to construct a long and exhaustively-argued appeal to his institute for a raise, complete with mathematical tables about comparative salaries.

Underneath Milena's gushings, her picture of Kafka sounds all too like Dickens's memorably manipulative "eternal child" Harold Skimpole in *Bleak House*.

You could argue that, somehow, his TB has utterly changed Kafka's character, but this would be pretty ridiculous. Kafka has always had a distinct tendency to act otherworldy when it suits him. Back in 1912, when he famously depicts the wretched female workers in the asbestos factory, there is, in his baffled description of the filth and the noise and the almost dehumanized women, no sign that this factory actually *belongs to him*, that he is any way responsible for the situation (not to mention, hoping to profit from it). We've already seen his innocent-sounding but blatantly ludicrous travel plans for Felice. On August 15, 1913, he told Felice that they must "salve" poor, sick (!) Hermann's fears by telling him they won't need his financial support—but she'll have to do it because "I have no proper understanding of money."

It looks very much as if he presented himself to young, intense, unhappy, arty Milena in just this well-practiced way, acting the innocent abroad in the big bad world.

Kafka's own stories and private notes show that he knew what his own game was. "The Judgment" is centered on the revelation that George was "always actually an innocent child" but "more actually" a devilish person *because* he was childlike for too long. Kafka privately called himself "devilish in all innocence" at the breakup with Felice in 1914 (when Grete showed her his treacherous letters).

In other words, he knew very well that if a man appears *too* innocent about the business of living, we should count our spoons when he arrives—and maybe lock up our daughters, too.

However, there's nothing innocent about his letter to Milena on August 9. This letter is perhaps the most famous of them all. It's quoted in every single book on Kafka as a piece of terrifying honesty, a brave attempt by a troubled man to explain his dark inner world to the woman he hopes can save him from it.

A Little Something

In this best known of all his many letters, Kafka tells Milena about his first-ever night of sex and how this led to the troubles she encountered with him in the Vienna woods (I've preserved Kafka's breathless punctuation and one curious slide of tense):

> in the hotel she all innocently did a tiny vile something (not worth talking about), said a little dirty something (not worth talking about), but the memory remained, I knew right then that I'll never forget it* and at the same time I knew or believed I knew that this vileness and dirtiness, outwardly unconnected with the whole thing, was inwardly very necessarily connected with it and that this vileness and dirtiness (of which her little deed and her little word had been the little sign to me) was exactly what had pulled me with such insane power into this hotel, which I would have otherwise avoided with all my power. And it always stayed the way it was then. My body, often quiet for years, would then be shaken again to the point of unbearability by this yearning for a little, for a quite specific vileness, for something mildly repugnant, painful, dirty, even in the best of this that there was for me there was something of it, a bad little smell, a bit of sulfur, a touch of hell.

This story is generally taken as biographical fact—the brave confession of a man passionate about Milena but also passionate about the truth at all costs.

The truth, as you'll have guessed, is something very different.

---

*This unnerving drop into the future tense is a bit like the sudden swoop to the present in the first paragraph of *The Castle* (as restored in Pasley's Critical Edition): "K. stood for long time on the wooden bridge which *leads* from the country road to the village . . ." (My italics). Here, as there, Kafka uses it to hammer home the *reality* of the situation.

Telling It Straight?

Context, as usual, is everything. Kafka's great confession to Milena doesn't come out of the blue and it isn't powered by love. He writes it down during the miniature storm of letters to her on August 8–9, 1920. This is just after she's told him she's *not* going to leave her husband for him after all—and after she's evidently asked him why he felt such "fear" about meeting her again.

What's happened, under all the high-flown words, is fairly clear. Kafka has blown it and he knows it. In the month since their wonderful four days, Milena (as she was to write to Brod) had "telegraphed, telephoned, written, begged in the name of God" that he should come to see her in Vienna. But he didn't. Instead of boldly coming to claim her as his, he dusted off his well-worn train timetables to propose a convenient meeting (she'd told him that her husband had threatened to "beat and throttle" him, which may have had something to do with it). Now she's more or less telling him that she can't handle his fear.

Kafka has just suffered the greatest (perhaps, the only serious) rejection of his life. For the first time, he has truly wanted a real woman and truly believed he has won her—he's just dumped his fiancée for her!—only to be told that she's had massive second thoughts. And it's clear to him that these doubts are to do with his "fear" of sex.

(Milena, herself, backs this up: later, she wrote to Brod that she had ruined it all because she was too much of an earthly, earthy woman of bodily desires. She couldn't agree to give up her husband and bow to a life of "strictest asceticism." However much she loved Kafka and his writing, she wanted him to do more than write letters and stare into her eyes as if he couldn't breathe or as if his feet hurt).

This is the mood in which he writes his famous "confession" to

Milena. Kafka has just been rejected in terms no man likes to hear. And since he was a human who hurt like a human, we should maybe take a closer look before we accept his reaction as an objective report from his life.

Two Big Bangs

In the "Letter to His Father" (written a year earlier), Kafka had blamed his father's casual reference to brothels for first setting up in his teenage head the idea of his "dirtiness." Now, in his "Letter to [still married] Milena," Kafka blames his first actual night with a girl for having caused his fixation on "a quite specific vileness."

In other words, Kafka gives two completely different stories about how he came to eat the apple that left him feeling sex was dirty. Now, both versions of this fall from innocence simply cannot be true. You can't identify *two* psychological big bangs in your life, years apart, and claim them both as a cause of the same problem—without undermining each.

Kafka seems to be tailoring his alleged psycho-history very much according to the recipient. Whatever he claimed to Milena, we know that his sexual tastes were not created overnight, and they weren't confined to a "quite specific" little peccadillo. He admitted to Grete Bloch that the sight of her fur stole made him uncomfortable and that he'd often been troubled by the same accessory in his sisters' wardrobes. In September 1907, he wrote to Hedwig Weiler that "furs hide a scared girl too much and they want too much to be admired for themselves, and to cause pain." His drastically masochistic images of being stabbed or sliced up by knives are so well known that they hardly need be quoted again. An even more shocking vision pops up in the diaries of 1911 (October 30), as the vegetarian Kafka dwells on the thought of breaking his own laws in an orgy of meat-eating and anal punishment:

I stuff the long slabs of smoked rib-meat into my mouth without biting them and then drag them out from behind, ripping them through my stomach and guts.

It's highly unlikely that one night with a streetwalker, however unbridled she may have been, would have led to all this—not to mention, an apparent fixation on womens' tight-laced apron strings.[4]

But if Kafka's famous confession of August 9, 1920, *isn't* autobiographical fact, what on earth *is* it?

To see this, we'll have to look at the whole story, not just the section that is always quoted.

The Pornographic Melodrama[5]

I remember my first night. We lived in the Zeltnergasse at that time and opposite us was a sweet shop, a salesgirl was always standing in the doorway, I wandered about upstairs, a little over twenty years old, up and down in the room never stopping busy with the nerve-racking cramming of meaningless things for [my] state examination. It was in summer, very hot, that time of year, it was quite unbearable, I stopped again and again at the window with horrible Roman law between my teeth, at last we made an arrangement using sign language. I was to pick her up at 8 o'clock but when I went down that evening, another man was already there, well that didn't change anything, I was afraid of the whole world, so I was afraid of this man, too, even if he hadn't been there I would *still* have been afraid of him. But though the girl did take his arm, she made a sign to me that I should follow them. And so we came to the Schützeninsel [a park] and drank beer there, me at the next table, then left, myself following, slowly to the girl's apartment, somewhere around the meat market, the man said good-bye there, the girl hurried into the house, I waited a while until she came out to me again and then we went to a hotel on the Kleinseite [across the river]. That was all nerve-racking, exciting and vile, even before the hotel and in the hotel it was no different. And when toward morning, it was still hot and fine, we crossed the Charles Bridge on our way home, I was certainly happy, but this happiness consisted simply in at last having some respite from the eternal clamoring of my body, above all the happiness consisted of the whole thing not having been *even more* vile and *even more* dirty. I was with the girl one time after that, I think it was 2 nights later, everything was just as good as the first time, but I went straight out to the countryside afterward, messed around a bit with a girl, and when I got back to Prague I couldn't stand the sight of the salesgirl, I never said a word to her, she was (from my point of view) my wicked enemy and yet she was a good humored, friendly girl, she kept on following me with her uncomprehending eyes. I won't say that the only reason for my enmity was (because it certainly wasn't) that in the hotel she all innocently did a tiny vile something (not worth talking about), said a little dirty something (not worth talking about), but the memory remained, I knew right then that I'll never forget it and at the same time I knew or believed I knew that this vileness and dirtiness, outwardly unconnected with the whole thing, was inwardly very necessarily connected with it and that this vileness and dirtiness (of which her little deed and her little word had been the little sign to me) was exactly what had pulled me with such insane power into this hotel, which I would have otherwise avoided with all my power.

And it always stayed the way it was then. My body, often quiet for years, would then be shaken again to the point of unbearability by this yearning for a little, for a quite specific vileness, for something mildly repugnant, painful, dirty, even in the best of this that there was for me there was something of it, a bad little smell, a bit of sulfur, a touch of hell.

The hot evening, the bored a young man studying for his professional future, the repeated interruptions and stares from the
middle-class window down to the salesgirl below, the secret,
wordless sign language of assignation—surely this is a set of stock
fin-de-siècle erotic images?

It could almost be a setup from Schnitzler's brilliant, notorious, and oft-banned *Reigen (La Ronde)*, a play which Kafka certainly knew and (unlike most of Schnitzler's work) admired.

The husbandlike figure behind whose back the girl gives signals
seems all too convenient, given who Kafka is writing to. The repeti-
tion of "little" (it occurs six time in his description of whatever it was
that went on in the hotel) starts to sound distinctly fixated. In fact, it
all starts to feel more like pornographic writing than objective recall.
After all, porn-speak today is filled with buzz-words like *dirty*, *nasty*,
little, and *naughty*—just as it was, no doubt, in Kafka's day (Joyce
makes Leopold Bloom helplessly excited at the mere words *naughty*
and *young*).

And something is *missing* from Kafka's supposedly true-life tale
of disastrous sexual initiation. What's *not* there is the thing that *all*
pornographers suppress when they write about their hells and
heavens.[6] It's the lie that is essential to the "pornographic idyll" in
which the girls are always (however inexplicably) eager to party
just as much as the men. Look again: there's no mention or hint
from Kafka of the *act of payment* that no doubt took place in one
way or another. In other words, the really central fact of Kafka's
story—that his first experience of sex was *paid* sex, with all which
that implies—is covered up by the storyteller, just as the language
of the day drew a tactful veil over the well-known reality of such
things by using phrases like *sweet maidens* and *chambre séparée*.

But this story isn't all that Kafka confesses to on August 9. In
the same letter (quoted far less often), Kafka informs Milena that he
planned "by night and day" to seduce the chambermaid in the hotel
at Merano. Later, he found that a "a very willing girl ran into my

hands" whose words he "more or less had to translate into my own language." This, remember, is Kafka writing to a girl who is *literally* his translator, whom he merrily invited to come to this very same hotel and whose rent he offered to pay if she left her husband.

Was it all true? Did he really "plan by day and night" to seduce the maid? Did he really get another "willing" (non-German) girl?

If it's true, it means that Kafka in 1920 was (though ill, engaged to Julie, and passionately writing to Milena) a compulsive seducer of servant-class girls. If he's making it all up, it means that he's clearly capable of inventing shocking "truths" about himself as part of an emotional campaign.

A spectacular true confession or a pretty extraordinary example of vengeful story-telling? Either way, it hardly fits the picture Milena later greatly helped to paint—that of a man simply too sensitive and honest for this world.

A Fair, Unsullied Soul

One of Kafka's extraordinary "Zürau Aphorisms" implies that the *gaze* of a woman is a good thing but the *sex* that results is bad: "And thus Good has tempted us into Evil, the gaze of the woman has tempted us into her bed." This predates his panicked staring into Milena's eyes in the Vienna woods by about two years and it suggests a consistent line in his tormented sexuality.

The question is *why* Kafka should have been so tormented by the sight of Milena's naked young flesh. After all, he didn't seem to have much trouble, a dozen years earlier, enjoying looking at sweet Hansi's boyish body or popping off to the *chambre séparée* at the Trocadero with a large and busty blonde.

The passage of time is again central here, because the most interesting and revealing thing of all about Kafka's sexual torment is its *history*.

The fact is that there is no sign whatever of such torment in the early letters to Brod. Whatever Kafka later decided (and persuaded himself of, and wrote to Milena and sort-of wrote to his father), this disgust and guilt about sex is—as we saw earlier—simply not part of his salad days as a reader of *The Amethyst,* beau-about-town, and frequenter of the Trocadero.

In other words, Kafka's famous sexual angst is not something he was born with, or had scared into him by his father at an early age, or got fixated on thanks to one too-memorable night with a dirty-talking good-time girl. It is something that *came about* as Kafka got older and found himself faced with either growing out of his youthful sexual tastes (perfectly acceptable then in a young man-about-town) or taking the consequences (a lonely old age paying for sex).

As a middle-aged man by now, Kafka understandably found it impossible to admit to his "dirty" sexual tastes, honed in youth by brothels, streetwalkers, good-time girls, graphic porn, and unusual reading-matter, when he was at last with a woman who (unlike Felice or Julie) he truly, madly desired, who was his intellectual equal, who seemed to love him, and especially who seemed to love and understand what he himself saw as the most important thing about him—his writing.

This is a genuinely tragic moment from literary history—a moment where a great filmmaker could easily make the audience want to leap up and shout, "Just *tell* her! Just *trust* her!" A moment like the wonderful, horrible scenes in Chekhov, in which people *don't* say the vital thing that could have made a new life possible.

And Kafka *does* try to tell Milena about what he actually likes doing, in that letter—but he simply can't bring himself to go the whole way. Just as he couldn't write about "I" having sex with Frieda in *The Castle*, he now can't tell Milena what he actually likes doing. All he can do is hint, in a story.

What *is* the dirty little thing that (allegedly) happened that night and which now—however it came about—rules his sexuality? We don't know and shouldn't care. What matters is that, whatever it is, Kafka quite literally *cannot* say it to a decent girl. He can't escape from the old pornographic melodrama where a girl is either a night-clubbing, good-time Hansi (with whom the dirty side of a man does dirty stuff) or a married, literary, middle-class Milena (with whom the pure side of a man does pure stuff), and never the twain shall meet. "I am dirty, Milena, endlessly dirty, that's why I shout so loudly about purity" (August 20, 1920).

Kafka doesn't want the world to be like that. But he can't get beyond it without someone else holding his hand. Just as happened with Felice and his fantasy home life, Kafka needs Milena to make the vital move, to tell him it's all right *before* he even says what he's getting at but doesn't quite dare write (never mind say). He needs her to guarantee *in advance* that whatever he does will be okay.

Like his man from the country, Kafka can't make the leap of faith without being told it's okay to do so—which means, of course, that it isn't a leap of faith at all. Imagine a movie hero saying to his girl, "Yes! I'll risk telling you everything—so long as you promise in advance that it'll be all right." It would be absurd; it would belong in comedy (which is all about stasis), not drama (which is all about change). If nothing's truly risked, nothing can really happen. As another of Kafka's wonderful images puts it: If you climb the ladder, yes, you might fall, but if you don't climb it, guess what? You still end up on the ground—and not maybe, but for sure.

Although she later claimed to bitterly regret it, Milena in real time was (quite understandably) not prepared to put her entire married life on the line to give Kafka the blank emotional check he needed before jumping on the train to Vienna. They did meet up shortly after this letter, but it's clear their sneaked weekend was not a success. The letters afterward speak of "lies" and they never met as lovers again, leaving Kafka alone once again and Milena with a sense of regret and guilt that led her to tell the world what a pure, innocent, and sensitive genius had loved and lost her.

Kafka's mind-set, which seems to have doomed the relationship, is very common indeed in the male imagination. The story of the bad girl you lust for versus the good girl you love is one of our most often-used motors of fiction, written and filmed, Hollywood or Bollywood. It's the same theme that Brod treated farcically in his soft-porn tale for *The Amethyst*, about a man who manages to arrange things so perfectly that he can actually have sex with his curvaceous wench while simultaneously talking to his real girlfriend. It's hardly a *complex* dilemma, though, or one that deserves vast reams of psychological theorizing.

Saying that you are impure and dirty does not make you profound. In fact, stripped of genuine religious belief (which would involve real self-mortification and penitence), this vision of the soul-scape is frankly banal. James Joyce has Leopold Bloom indulge in a comic, contemporary version of exactly the same comfortable, modern self-flagellation as he adjusts his wet shirt following his unilateral virtual encounter with crippled Gerty MacDowell: "What a brute he had been! At it again? A fair unsullied soul had called to him and, wretch that he was, how had he answered?"

Yes, Kafka was uneasy about his sexual tastes, but if feeling more at ease with bad girls than with nice girls (and feeling bad about it afterward) is a sign of potential sainthood, there are an awful lot of men in line waiting for halos.

VII

WHY THE MYTH MUST GO

The most famous story of the twentieth century.

Even if the K.-myth is nonsense, why does that *matter?*

We'll see why if we look at Kafka's most famous image, his beetle—if it is indeed *Kafka's* beetle at all.

To find out, we'll leave Prague and go to Weimar, the place where, in the summer of 1912, Kafka played at being Faust to real young Gretchen, and where he twice noted the open-air theater laid out by the greatest figure in German literature, at the very time he stood between drafts of *Amerika,* which culminates in a strange vision of an impossibly wonderful . . . open-air theater.

Goethe's Beetle, or The Unbearable Blindness of Kafka Studies

Everyone (including millions who've never read the story and never will) knows *The Metamorphosis* as *the story about a man who gets turned into a beetle.* It's quite simply the most famous high-concept literary vision of the twentieth century.

The image seems to burst into the world unheralded on November 18, 1912, from nowhere, from the sunless depths of Kafka's subconscious, born out of either the timeless, Freudian struggle between himself and his father, his sense of Jewish self-hatred, his relationship with Felice, or his mystical foreseeing of the Holocaust. Or something like that.

In fact, it comes from none of these.

Kafka's most famous image came not out of the blue, but from the work of the most dominant figure in German literature, the man with whom Kafka (who was anything but modest in his literary benchmarks) felt himself to have "an exceptionally intimate relationship"[1]—Johann Wolfgang von Goethe.

It's hard to describe to a modern Anglo-Saxon reader Goethe's status within German culture in Kafka's day. If you think of him as Germany's Shakespeare, Dickens, Keats, Byron, and perhaps Benjamin Franklin, too, all rolled into one man, you get some idea. And from the end of 1911 right through 1912, Kafka, always concerned with Goethe, was practically obsessed with him, as can be see in his diary.

On Christmas Day 1911, Kafka wrote of German literature's "boundless dependence" on Goethe's prose and famously concluded that "through the might of his work, Goethe probably holds back the development of the German language." We find him two weeks later believing that "I have been totally and utterly under Goethe's influence this week, have just exhausted the power of that influence and have therefore become useless"; at the end of the month, he finds that books about Goethe bring on "a diffuse, completely unusable excitement" and plans an essay on "Goethe's terrifying nature"; on February 4 he reads books about Goethe "with a zeal that goes right through me and holds me back from any writing," but next day he's so tired that he has "even" given up reading Goethe's vast autobiography and instead looks at "Goethe's handsome silhouette." On the eighth, he notes Goethe's remark that "my pleasure in bringing things out was boundless." On the thirteenth, he prepares himself for writing a speech, like an athlete warming up his muscles, by "reading lines of Goethe as though I were running along the intonations with my entire body." On March 17, he writes down lines from of Goethe's "Consolation ·in Suffering," having heard a musical version.

In summer 1912 comes a completely Goethe-centered trip to Weimar, during which Kafka not only does the full highbrow Goethe-tourist itinerary, postcards and all, but (as we've seen) casts himself as Faust to the young, innocent Gretchen of the house in a real-life seduction adventure. After that, it's off to the Jungborn Sanatorium, where the now soon-to-be-published Kafka discusses "the unhappy Goethe who made so many people unhappy" with a land surveyor who is trying to convert him to Christianity, and dreams of Goethe "declaiming with infinite freedom and whim" (July 14, 1912).

In his period of dithering before first writing to Felice, he spends an evening listening to Ottla reading Goethe's poetry ("chosen with real feeling"), goes through old diaries, and uses one of Goethe's most often quoted lines about Faust (turned boldly into a negative) to depict his own state of mind (August 15, 1912).*

Now, given the extraordinary status of Goethe in German culture generally at this time, Kafka's obviously special interest in him during 1912, and the countless studies done of Kafka's "bug story," it would be pretty amazing if that central image of *The Metamorphosis* were actually to be found in some little-known comment of Goethe's, yet had gone unnoticed in all these years, wouldn't it?

The truth is far more extraordinary.

---

*Goethe has God say of Faust that a good man, even in his dark times, "is well aware what way ahead is right" ("*ist sich des rechten Weges wohl bewusst*"). Kafka writes that he is "unaware what way ahead is right" ("*des rechten Weges bin ich mir auch nicht bewusst*.")

A Beetle Seeking Nourishment

Kafka's image of a man (the hero of the story, in fact) imagining himself being turned into a large beetle comes not from some obscure work, but from the book that made Goethe's career; the first modern multinational bestseller in literary history; a novel that was blamed for such a pan-European suicide cult that the author felt obliged to add the warning, "Be a man and do not follow me"; the young Napolean Bonaparte's favorite book, a work of fiction studied by every nineteenth-century German grammar school boy (including Kafka) and which Kafka had reread in 1911.

The book in question is *The Sorrows of Young Werther*, a work so internationally famous that even though Goethe lived and wrote for a further normal human lifetime, his obituary in *The Times* still referred to him as "the author of *Werther*."

Werther thinks about being turned into a beetle. And he doesn't think this in some obscure corner of the work. This fantasy is described in the *very first* of the letters that make up the epistolary novel. It's thus no exaggeration at all to say that the following passage would have been read and at least theoretically studied by *every educated German-speaker* of Kafka's day:

> One would like to turn into a june bug [*Maienkäfer*] so that one could swim around in this sea of pleasant scents, getting all one's nourishment [*Nahrung*] like this.

It's not just striking that Werther (literature's most famous suicide) dreams about turning into a beetle—it's *why* he does. He wants to change, in order to find some mysterious, unearthly *nourishment*. The German word Goethe uses *(Nahrung)* is one of the most loaded of Kafka's words in *The Metamorphosis* (it's also central to his later stories "A Hunger-Artist" and "Investigations of a Dog.")

In a climatic and extraordinarily moving scene, Kafka—for the only time in his whole story—suggests that there may be, at some level, *some* kind of positive, spiritualizing aspect to Gregor's metamorphosis. Here, Gregor creeps out from his room (for the last time) to listen to his sister's violin playing:

> Was he an animal, if music touched him like this? He felt as though he were being shown the path to that longed-for, unknown nourishment [*Nahrung*]*

Werther and Gregor both dream of somehow sidestepping the tough business of living and deriving pure, sensual *nourishment* (from scents and music, respectively).

Let's be plain about what we have here. This is the cultural equivalent of two generations of English scholars simply *not noticing* that James Joyce has quoted the start of *Hamlet* at the start of *Ulysses*. This is unthinkable. It could never happen. People reading *Ulysses* would be bound to have noticed by now—precisely *because* there is no great Joyce myth that stands in the way of their reading.

There can be no clearer evidence that the K.-myth quite literally makes people—even highly educated German scholars—*incapable of reading what Kafka actually wrote.*

A King in Underpants

On the fateful night when Kafka met Felice, she made only one remark (he reported later) that he didn't like. This was when Brod's father said he'd show them a picture of Goethe in his underwear, and Felice quoted a popular play: "He's remains a king,

---

*Because this is Kafka, the hero is, of course, utterly deluded and his fantasy immediately turns into a deeply disturbing vision in which he would protect his sister and send her to the conservatory—upon which she'd burst into moved tears and he'd "raise himself up to her shoulders and kiss her neck" (still as a beetle).

even in his underwear." Kafka disliked this so much that he "almost felt a pressure in my throat" and should (he says) have asked himself why he felt so strongly about it.

So why *did* Kafka feel so strongly? Well, what's the central, unforgettable image of "The Judgment" ("her" story, as he often called it later)? It's a senile-seeming father figure prancing about with his underwear visible, yet "still a giant."

We're so used to plodding biographical criticism ("Oh, look, a father figure, well, obviously, this means Hermann Kafka") that everyone has missed something far more interesting.

Kafka's first great story talks about an abortive revolt by a man who has never fully developed. The revolt is carried out in an act of *writing* (the letter to his friend) and is against a terrible, overshadowing figure in a nightshirt and dirty underwear, who yet is still a giant. And this is in a story created *just* after he had finally decided to write to the woman who had made his throat tighten by talking about Goethe remaining "a king even in his underwear."

Even the *language* is the same: in German, Georg looks up at the "*Schreckbild*" (vision of terror) that is his father. In January that same year, Kafka wanted to write about Goethe's "*schreckliche*" nature.

If people had simply taken Kafka at his own word when he said (as he so often did) that *literature* was the most important thing to him, surely they would have noticed the mighty presence of Goethe at the heart of both "The Judgment" and *The Metamorphosis*?

It's the K.-myth, with its mania for a rose-tinted obsession with Kafka's emotional and family life, that is to blame for this incredible blindness of Kafka scholars. Obsessed with biography—with a highly selective biography, too—entire generations of them have simply *not seen* the great Goethe when he is before their very noses in Kafka's actual *writing*.

Who knows what other secrets of Kafka's texts might leap into focus if we could only begin to read them straight, without being fogged by the K.-myth of his life and by its secret twin, the theoreticians' myth of infinite complexity?

I suggest we need a brand-new theory of how to read Kafka's writing. The oldest theory of all. The theory used by Kafka's first readers, who—lucky them!—knew nothing of Felice, Milena, Hermann Kafka, the diaries, deconstruction, structuralism, postmodernism, or (especially lucky them) the Holocaust.

That theory is, of course, no theory at all. The readers who first realized that Kafka was something special read his writing by reading it.

We can't read Kafka's writing in this innocent way. The trouble with being human (as Adam and Eve found out) is that you can't *un*know things. Since we inescapably know things about Kafka, the only option we have is to know them properly.

This is clearest when we come to the last and possibly the biggest hurdle for readers: the assumption that Kafka takes us into bizarre worlds.

The Bizarre Worlds of Franz Kafka

Now, this one looks hard to deny on the face of it. A man arrested for nothing? A man turning up in a village and being told he needs permission from its castle just to stay the night? A man turned into a beetle?

Well, we've already discussed the beetle. It turns out to be a literary device with a high-class pedigree. And as for *The Trial* and *The Castle*, they should come equipped with a sticker on the cover saying "Anglo-Saxon readers beware."

But surely literature is literature is literature? This whole book has argued that we don't *need* to know anything about Dr. Kafka's life and loves and so on, hasn't it?

Certainly it has. I deny absolutely that we need to know anything about Kafka the man. His first readers and reviewers knew nothing about him, and we don't know need it, either. *They* liked his stuff purely as literature, and so can we. But what they *did* have was knowledge *shared with* Kafka. The air of the times. The spirit of the day. They inhabited the same world as he did. We don't—and it can lead us into gross misunderstandings of his works.

In other words, to start reading *The Trial* without knowing certain basic things—not things about Kafka the *man*, but about his *world*—is like going to *Hamlet* without knowing, as every groundling in Shakespeare's England knew without even thinking about it, that when a king dies, a legitimate prince whose uncle illegally grabs the crown must be in daily fear of assassination. Or reading *The Unbearable Lightness of Being* ignorant of what the Red Army was and did. Or picking up *Extremely Loud and Incredibly Close* having never heard of 9/11.

Of course, you *could* tackle any of these works like that, as simple constructions of words. Each would have passages that worked by the sheer quality of their vision and writing, but whether you would have much idea what kind of book you were reading is another matter.

Arrested for Nothing

Every Anglo-Saxon reader opening *The Trial* feels that he or she is immediately being hurled into a bizarre world. A man is arrested at home, examined by an official, then allowed to go about his normal business while still being obliged to attend court hearings (only preliminary ones at first, with the main trial not yet even given a starting date)—and all without any crime being named or charge being brought. Where can we possibly be, if not in some bizarre fantasy world?

Well, there's a place where all the above was perfectly possible in Kafka's day and still is now. The strange and bizarre parallel world called Europe.

The horrible story of the missing girl in Portugal (still ongoing at the time of writing) has made Anglo-Saxon readers aware of the workings of a legal world very unlike ours. In Europe, today, it's perfectly possible to be a publicly named suspect, under official investigation for a terrible crime, without ever being charged or locked up. Not only possible, but perfectly normal, because in Europe today, just as in Kafka's day, the legal system is *inquisitorial* rather than (as in the United States, the United Kingdom, and its former dominions) *adversarial*.

Anglo-Saxon theory is that the truth will come out from citizens' arguing against one another, with expert help if they want it (and can afford it), the argument to be decided by twelve ordinary good men and true, with the state's role merely to be a neutral arbiter of the punishment handed out to the loser.

The classic European theory is based on very different ideas. Here, the state, which is assumed to be the highest authority, will send in its agents to actively and objectively seek out the truth. An examining magistrate's job, essentially the same all over Continental Europe, is to decide whether there is a case worth the state's pursuing at all. To find this out, he is empowered to openly place people under investigation and (if he thinks it necessary) even to arrest them for days, weeks, months before a charge is brought or even named (if it ever is).

As one modern German introduction to German law puts it:

> It is unavoidable that the rights of people who are legally innocent are thus impinged upon . . . often, persons who suffer enforcement measures in the course of a criminal proceeding are materially innocent. The police and the state advocates are obliged to follow every serious path of inquiry, which quite inevitably leads to suspicion falling on people who have nothing to do with the deed under investigation.

(This aspect of European law was systematically abused in the best of causes by the Italian state in the late 1980s: unable to get Mafia godfathers to trial due to a lack of living witnesses, brave judges deliberately ordered endless public precharge examinations of their affairs, just to make life and business hard for them. This would have been quite impossible in Great Britain or the United States.)

In Germany today, once they've been examined (before they're accused of anything, remember) in a preliminary trial (*Ermitt-lungsverfahren*) a person may then be accused and brought to a middle trial (*Zwischenverfahren*) at which the case against them is examined in detail. Only then does the main trial (*Hauptverhand-lung*) start. It is a principle that "the only people who should appear as accused in a main trial are those whose condemnation is distinctly more likely than their acquittal."[2]

If you imagine these genuine, modern German concepts and terms being translated into English in a novel, you'll see how even a real, modern Continental legal system can easily seem bizarrely loaded against the individual to Anglo-Saxon ears (just as, to Continental eyes, the Anglo-Saxon system seems impossibly skewed in favor of wealthy individuals).

So when we pick up *The Trial,* we should remember that Kafka lived under (and was trained in) a legal system very foreign to ours, with a fundamentally different conception of the relationship between individual and state. What we read as bizarre is actually not nearly so far as we might think from the actual reality of Kafka's own world.

This is vital to see at another point early in *The Trial.* Kafka lived in a country that had elections and parliaments but was, underneath, nothing like what we would call a democracy.

The Kaiser had the legal right to pass laws without any consent from Parliament. His power was maintained not by any popular consent but (as it was said) by his four armies: the standing army, the sitting army (the bureaucracy that absorbed a third of all government revenues), the kneeling army (the Church, ever-loyal), and the creeping army (of informers and spies).

Franz Josef regularly had to impose military law in peacetime to stop his peoples fighting each other, especially in Prague—it happened there for the last time in 1913. The tentacles of state power reached into everyday life. Any public meeting had to have a state official present to observe and note proceedings. Anyone applying for any job could be asked (as Kafka was) to produce (as Kafka did) a "Certificate of Good Behavior" from the police. Simply *not having anything against* you on the records ("negative vetting" as it's called) wasn't enough in the Habsburg Empire. You had to have a statement ("positive vetting") that the authorities considered you okay.

We tend to see the Habsburg Empire in a rosy light. Compared with its local successors, Fascism, Nazism, and Stalinism, no doubt anything looks pretty good. But no one knew those bad days were coming and, to its own thinking citizens, this empire was famously a "despotism tempered by incompetence."

And when Kafka started *The Trial*, and when he first read it aloud, there would have been another small matter on people's minds. Kafka began the novel on or about August 11, 1914. Just after Austria had gone and kicked off the Great War, in other words.

When Kafka's first listeners heard about Josef K.'s arrest, why did they laugh? They laughed for the same reason people laugh when they see the smug man walking happily toward the unseen banana skin. They laughed because they knew more than Josef K. did and could see he was an idiot about to get hurt.

When he's arrested, Josef K. thinks to himself: "K. lived in a free country,[3] everything was peaceful, all the laws stood firm." No doubt this was one of the passages where Kafka's first listeners burst out laughing. They could hardly have failed to see that K. was a seriously deluded man. More subtly deluded, perhaps, than Gregor Samsa is deluded when he plans to go to work as a beetle, but deluded.

Josef K. an Everyman plunged into a bizarre world? No. A deluded character in an exaggerated—but still recognizable—version of *this* world. And his first listeners would hardly have failed to note that joining Kafka's own first name and his hero's first name yields the pregnant combination Franz Josef.

This isn't a fantasy, it's black social comedy. This is even more clear when we come to Kafka's other great novel.

Surveying the Land, 1922

A man turns up at a village pub and is told that he needs official permission to stay there, from bureaucrats who work for the local lord in his low-rise castle on high. Once again, we seem to be thrown into the realms of bizarre fantasy. Surely, the villagers' superstitious awe and even fear of mysterious powers-that-be who can ruin your life in nebulous ways is pure Kafka?

Here's an example of the way the fearful villagers think:

> It's better not to ask questions, because questions arouse the suspicions of the village mayor . . . A man has to live in such a way that his name never reaches the ear of the authorities. If it does, they write it down and then that man is in for a lot of trouble later on.

Except that this is not Kafka but a modern Honduran farmer quoted in *The Independent*.[4] No mystery, no fantasy: for millions of people, this is the reality of how power works, even today. As Brod's story "Reasonable Force" (*Notwehr*) put it in the very same anthology where "The Judgment" appeared, "Everyone in the village was supposed to fear the strict, merciful Lord whom they had never seen."*

At the risk of stating the obvious, throughout European his-

---

*This story contains many other images that are reminiscent of those in *The Trial*. But the idea that Kafka might have been influenced *as a writer* by Brod doesn't fit in with the K.-myth, so no one has even bothered with them.

tory the ruling classes have lived in and governed from places called "castles." It's crazy to ignore this foghorn hint of meaning in the book. And the fact that Kafka's castle doesn't look like one shouldn't fool us. Real modern castles don't *have* to look like castles. Prague Castle is a case in point. An even clearer one is Dublin Castle. This is the place that was, in Kafka's day, the heart of British semimilitary rule over Ireland. It looks, as any visitor to Leopold Bloom's city will know, nothing whatever like a picture-book "castle." But it *is* one, it was *called* one, and it *functioned as* one—that is, as a modern center of power and control.

So when Kafka says that his castle doesn't much *look like* a castle, he doesn't mean it *isn't* a castle, he means it's a *real* castle that doesn't have to give a damn what it *looks like* so long as people keep on respecting it as "the castle."

And as for needing permission to stay: this seems bizarre to Anglo-Saxons. Any government in Britain or America which tried to pass a new law forcing all citizens to report to the local police station or courthouse, within days, every time they moved house or even rented a room, on pain of a substantial fine, would be out of office next day. If they nevertheless managed to enact it, they would face vast demonstrations (and in some U.S. states, no doubt, armed insurrection). But this is the perfectly normal way of things in Germany and Austria right now, never mind in Kafka's day.

In those days, in rural Austria just as in rural Britain, the local magistrate was very often also the local landowner. If you had turned up as a mysterious and well-dressed stranger in (say) backwoods Galicia in 1914, the nearest social bigwig is exactly who the loyal pub keeper would have notified.

And if you had turned up saying you were a "land surveyor"?

Kafka in 1922 had recently become (without any enthusiasm) a citizen of a brand-new would-be nation that had been drawn on a map at Versailles out of the chaos of a collapsed empire—and drawn with a high-handed (and eventually fatal) disregard for ethnic niceties.

This was happening all over Europe. Bohemia's Germans didn't want to be Czechs, many Romanians wanted to be Hungarians, and so on. In such a place and time, to make the hero of your novel a man whose job is to define boundaries of the basic human resource, land, makes him a figure absolutely loaded with hints of change and dislocation.

Think how a mysterious land surveyor would be received on the Ulster borders in 1920, in Bosnia in 1996, in Iraq today. As Orlando Figes notes, in neighboring Imperial Russia in Kafka's lifetime, reformist government land surveyors were driven off and even killed by peasants. An archaeologist friend of mine from Galway University, appearing with a theodolite in deepest Ireland in the early 1980s, was greeted with suspicion by two ancient bachelor farming brothers as a "sapper" (army engineer), which must have been a folk memory of the great British Army surveys of the 1840s, as immortalized in Brian Friel's wonderful *Translations.*

Land surveyors decide the basic issue of human social life ever since the first tribe laid claim to a certain waterfall where salmon leap, or a certain glade where berries grow: who *owns this*, who *belongs here* . . .

The Purpose of the Habsburg Empire

But surely we mustn't go too far here. Even in the informer-ridden Habsburg Empire there weren't *actually* courts in attics and mysterious castles you could never get into, were there? Of course not. Any more than there was *really* fog in the High Court of Chancery in Dickens's day.

Dickens, in *Bleak House*, simply and brilliantly makes the fog of legal argument into a real image. It's not just "like a fog" anymore—it actually *is* a fog. Kafka takes this same technique further. Instead of saying (as many people have said) that life is *like* a trial, Kafka makes it *literally* a trial—and refuses to ever let his hero out of the fog.

Reading *Bleak House* is excellent preparation for reading *The Trial*, which is perhaps not surprising. When he wrote *The Trial*, Kafka was still working now and again on *Amerika*, which he later called "straight imitation of Dickens." It's extremely unlikely that, when writing his legal-world novel, he didn't know very well that Dickens had written one, too. In fact, some of the images in *Bleak House* are very like those in *The Trial*. There, you'll find the strange attraction of the court to its victims; its false claims to glory and truth; the way it obsesses people, sucks the innocent into a case, gives them only insane dreams of some impossible judgment that will set *everything* right.

We find it incredibly hard to mentally grip the idea that Kafka's court isn't about equity, any more than the bureaucracy of Kafka's castle is about fair rulership. But this is because we are stuck in thinking of Kafka's works as some kind of religious-existential myths. As soon as we shake up our brain to see them as black social comedies, things become clear. As Dickens puts it in *Bleak House*:

> The one great principle of English law is to make business for itself . . . viewed in this light, it becomes a coherent scheme.

This should be printed across our mind when reading *The Trial* and *The Castle*. In those books, we get ramshackle, corrupt institutions that are simply their own justification. What's so complicated about that? What was the goal and purpose of the Habsburg Empire? To maintain and extend the Habsburg Empire, nothing more. In modern terms, what's the goal and purpose of the Microsoft Corporation?

The purpose of these institutions is simply to maintain themselves. Like Dickens's Court of Chancery, they dress up their sheer self-interest in robes and gowns and hierarchies to fool the people who allow them to keep existing. The only way to resist—as good John Jarndyce shows in *Bleak House*—is simply to walk away. Josef K. is told this explicitly: "The Court wants nothing from you; it takes you in if you come and it releases you if you go." But like Richard in *Bleak House*, he can't escape the idea that this mighty institution may, somehow, set everything right for him. As the pathetic Miss Flite puts it, in words that could come straight from *The Trial*, "I have the honor to attend court regularly. With my documents. I expect a judgment. Shortly. On the Day of Judgment."

I'm not suggesting that *The Trial* is an attack on Habsburg justice. Kafka's investigation is deeper than that. Where Dickens looks, with a Victorian reformer's stern but essentially hopeful eye, at the psychological effects of bad institutions, Kafka, in the more fundamentally troubled age of Freud and Nietzsche, shows us pure psychology—the psychology that *lets all such institutions flourish.*

Which brings us to the question Kafka himself famously asked: Was he an end or a beginning?

CONCLUSION:

AN END AND A BEGINNING

In tiefstem Schmerz geben wir bekannt, daß unser Sohn

JUDr. Franz Kafka

am 3. Juni im Sanatorium Kierling bei Wien, 41 Jahre alt, gestorben ist. Das Begräbnis findet am Mittwoch, den 11. Juni um ³/₄4 Uhr auf dem jüdischen Friedhof in Straschnitz statt.

PRAG, am 10. Juni 1924.

Hermann und **Julie Kafka,**
Eltern,
im Namen der trauernden Hinterbliebenen.

2392

Von Kondolensbesuchen bitten wir abzusehen.

A Czech Jew, German to the end.

There's simply no way that we can even start to go through the wonders of Kafka's works in any comprehensive way. That must be for another book. This one can only suggest a basic way of *approaching* that work—one that doesn't need any biographical knowledge or abstract theory.

The best thing is to read "The Judgment," that little story Kafka loved so much and which is the perfect introduction to his writing. So forget Kafka's father, forget Felice Bauer, forget Goethe, forget the Holocaust, forget Kafka's porn. See what Kafka actually *does* in this story.

The Judgment, or: A Mystery Beyond Sherlock Holmes

Georg Bendemann is about to get engaged. He's moving on in life and in the business he has now taken over running from his widowed father. He's writing about his engagement to a bachelor friend in Petersburg whose life is an emotional, business and social failure. Everything here, the descriptions and the psychology, seems perfectly realistic until we hear of a conversation with his fiancée about his friend: "if you have friends like that, Georg, you shouldn't have got engaged at all." Having written his letter, Georg goes—for no apparent reason and for the first time in months—to his father's room, to tell him about it.

Suddenly the realistic shell is cracked wide open and the world of raw emotions pours out.

His father accuses him of not feeling the loss of "our" mother, and of hiding things from him in business matters and of nebulous "unpleasant things." He then suggests that there is in fact, no friend in Petersburg.

This seems to be a factual point. Either Georg has a friend in Petersburg or not. In the normal run of stories we'd expect that the author would eventually reveal the answer, perhaps in a clever twist that will give us one of those "of course!" moments that all good detective stories deliver.

Kafka knows exactly what he's doing here. He's pulling us in by using the most modern and fashionable literary technique, one that he learned from a source we may find rather unlikely. But we have his own word for it in his diary entry for January 5, 1912, that Goethe-obsessed year in which he wrote "The Judgment":

> Löwy*, who suffers from terrible headaches, probably the early signs of a serious illness, was waiting for me in the street below, leaning on the wall of a house, his right hand pressed in despair to his forehead. I pointed him out to Weltsch[†], who leaned over from the sofa to the window. It seemed to me that for the first time in my life I was looking out of my window, down into the street, at an event which con-

*A penniless traveling Yiddish actor, at this time a protégé of Kafka's.

[†]Future editor of the Zionist journal *Self-Defense*, who arranged the first publication of Kafka's wonderful story "A Message from the Emperor" in 1919.

cerned me intimately and observing it in so light a manner. In principle I already know this way of observing things from Sherlock Holmes.

This passage is seldom quoted because it doesn't fit the K.-myth to have Kafka consciously employing the observational method of a highly-fashionable, fictional detective. But remember that in 1912, Detective Fiction was not the mass-market, popular mega-genre it is today. It was the latest literary style, a brand-new notion for a brand-new world, one that had been nurtured by Wilkie Collins, Dickens, Dostoyevsky and Conrad. And it is indeed the ideal genre for our post-religious world because in Detective Fiction, evil is revealed and punished, things are set right, not by the mill-wheels of the Lord, but by human reason. There *can* be Justice without God—what message could be more reassuring for a world after Darwin?

In "The Judgment," Kafka turns this new genre inside-out (just as he will in *The Trial*, which opens exactly like a detective story), setting out what will become his most essential creative thesis: that all this exact, reasoned observation *just doesn't deliver*.

Georg tries to hold onto his plan to "observe everything with absolute completeness," but this Sherlock Holmes-style rationality bounces clean off the real powerhouse of our lives, psychology. One minute, Georg's father claims his friend doesn't exist, the next minute he claims he *does* exist and is in fact spying for him on Georg himself. Logic seems to go right out of the window.

And so it does. That's the whole point. This is the non-mystery of "The Judgment." What is logically "true" or not is simply unimportant. Georg's father isn't "right"—he simply wins a battle of wills (hands down).

There's nothing complex at all about this. We all know it every day from our lives. Recall a time when you have seen a meeting being turned around, a domestic argument won, a social decision being reached. How did it happen? By someone arguing the point rationally, weighing up the pros and cons, proving to everyone else that their way was *logically right?* Or by someone putting their foot down, being ready to go on arguing all night, threatening to throw their toys out of the bath—*emotionally persuading* people to do things their way? A hundred to one it was the latter. What confuses us is that this result, which we all know from our *lives*, should appear *in a story*.

It's thus in "The Judgment" that Kafka first develops his secret weapon, a simple, daring and devastating one that he'll use again and again. It's the high-literary equivalent of a Sherlock Holmes story that looks and sounds exactly like a real proper Sherlock Homes story—except that all of Holmes's deductions lead absolutely nowhere. Kafka leaves us for dead with a killer sidestep that has driven his readers and critics to distraction for almost a century: his stories have all the *feel* of literature, but they simply refuse to deliver what we *expect* of literature.

Ever since the first Greek tragic actor opened his mouth at the moment of his character's utter ruin and uttered not a primal scream but poetry, we have expected our stories either to *end happily*—or to deliver some moral guidance about why they *didn't* end happily (and therefore *could have* ended happily if only the heroes had chosen differently).

We expect *consolation*—and we expect it so strongly that *expect* is not really the right word any more. It is more like a demand. Most authors (and almost all movies) give in to it. Kafka refuses that demand point blank. There is no salvation here. Georg Bendemann doesn't get what he deserves. He gets what he gets.

What makes us feel so sympathetic to Kafka's characters is that they—like us, his readers—*think* they live in a world that is run on grounds of morality and rationality, a world where there is some connection between what we *deserve* and what we *get*.

They expect a mysterious bureaucracy to be accessible (K.) or a court to be fair (Josef K.) or an argument to be settled by appeals to factual truth (Georg Bendemann) or an inherited illness to be curable by medicine (the country doctor) or that the door to the law should be open (the man from the country), or that just because the Emperor's message has been sent, it will ever get to you, or that the Promised Land will deliver its promises (Karl Rossmann).

They are all fatally, black-comically wrong. The clearest example is the best-known one, Gregor Samsa in *The Metamorphosis*. He's blatantly deluded about what is now possible for him and we know it. We know that he will *never get to work again*, forget about catching the next train if he hurries. But he has no *less* chance of getting to work on the train as a beetle than Josef K. has of getting "justice" from the Court or than K. has of getting into the Castle—because none of them has the slightest chance at all.

What makes Kafka's stories so memorable is the way he shows that the basic chasm between the world *we want* and the world *we're in* is as vast in the age of electric lights, cars and phones as it is in the Book of Job. And who needs a literary theory to tell them that?

And End or a Beginning?

Since Don Quixote started the whole business, our great prose stories have all been about the see-saw in our heads between rational worlds that can be drawn on a map and the psychologically decisive worlds in our heads. Peter Ackroyd's great biography of Dickens gives us a clue where Kafka fits into this tale—and why he quite rightly looms, to us, so large in it.

> In the nineteenth century Russian novelists, the material and the spiritual are in a certain sense interfused; and in the French novelists of the

nineteenth century it is the very genius of the material world to have no transcendental echoes: it remains splendidly itself. But in the work of Charles Dickens, the real and the unreal, the specific and the imagined, the mundane and the transcendental, exist in uneasy relation.

Kafka's roots were firmly in the nineteenth century—he experienced the twentieth, of course, but not as a man completely at home there. The twentieth century gave him (as it did many people) a feeling of wonder mixed with unease. To his observations of this new world, Kafka brought all three of the great traditions Ackroyd mentions above: he adored the realism of Stendhal and Flaubert; no one nowadays doubts his debt to Dostoyevsky's way of treating heightened psychological states: his early relationship to Dickens was (as we've seen) one of "straight imitation."

Kafka takes the novel to the next stage, as a simple example will show.

Richard in *Bleak House* ends up living virtually above his useless and manipulative solicitor, Vholes, so as to miss nothing of his case. Dickens makes Richard's situation still (just) physically realistic, and uses it to *symbolize* his psychological dependence on his lawyer. In *The Trial*, however, the wretched Block *literally* lives (impossibly) with his lawyer, for just the same reason.

Kafka has jumped clean over symbolic constructions. Psychological reality has become *the* reality. Dickens's court in *Bleak House* wreaks psychological havoc on people with its promises of material triumph so great (and so inexplicable) as to seem *almost* transcendental—but there is still always real money at stake in the background. Kafka's court induces the same psychological paralysis without ever having to tempt people: they tempt themselves because the court is nothing other than the image of their psychological need for absolute answers.

Kafka's way of telling also takes things to the next logical step. Dickens in *Bleak House* uses so many coincidences to get his characters where he wants them that his manipulations very nearly blow apart the "realistic" story. Kafka just does it straight, without blinking: *all* he wants is the psychological confrontations and he doesn't care who knows it. When Josef K. goes to the cathedral, the Chaplain is there simply because that's when and where Kafka wants him to be to say what Kafka wants him to say.

Kafka thus takes the novel one step further from Dickens and Dostoyevsky. He pushes the dominance of the "unreal" over the "real"—of psychological states over mappable facts—right to the limit. But he never over-steps that limit, though he comes perilously close in *The Castle. The Trial*, his greatest work, still has the unmistakable smack of a real place. This is what makes the story so endlessly wrong-footing.*

Kafka plays with the tension between psychology and reality like Brecht plays with theatrical belief and disbelief—and both of them do it by the sheer quality of their language. Brecht is the only literary author who can write a "folk-ballad" you actually believe came from nowhere, just as Kafka is the only one who can write a "legend" without it feeling blatant and artificial. The famous "alienation effect" only works because Brecht can indulge himself in it. He has the language to snap his fingers and make us re-suspend our disbelief in his characters whenever he feels like it. In any other writer's hands, the technique is dramatic suicide—an entire generation of 'sixties and 'seventies playwrights dashed their talents to pieces trying to get through a door that was only for one man. In the same way, only Kafka can take a dream-world so far without spiralling off into purely personal realms beyond all communication.

---

*Most scholars agree (on the evidence of the fragments) that Kafka at first planned an entire realistic strand to *The Trial* as well. But that part just never got off the ground. There's enough of it left, though, to give *The Trial* a feel of rooted-ness that *The Castle* just doesn't have.

The stop-you-dead truth and exactness of his observations—learned from his most illustrious literary predecessors (and, of course, Sherlock Holmes)—wrong-foots us every time. Just when we think we are lost in a purely symbolic, weightless place, Kafka flips us back into a world whose sights and thoughts we instantly (and gratefully) recognize. It is this that gives Kafka's works that haunting sense that *somewhere* in the inexplicable meanderings of the dream is a path that we should be able to rationally navigate.

Kafka takes the novel as far as it can go into the realms of purely psychological reality. Beyond him that road leads only to uncontrolled wallowing in personal visions—as all his endlessly banal imitators show.

And how does he make that balance work? Simple (like a perfect Olympic beam-routine is simple). No other writer has ever stayed so open to the call of his own personal vision while at the same time being so thoroughly and deliberately steeped—by years of conscious reading and thinking and practice—in all the tactics of literary storytelling. When the power was at last turned fully on (as it was in the Autumn of 1912) he was ready for it. To paraphrase Billie Wilder, when the Muse finally came calling, she knew where to find Franz Kafka: at his desk, at his place, where he always said he was supposed to be . . .

Why You Should Read Kafka Before You Waste Your Life

Kafka famously said "I am an end or a beginning." It turns out that he was half-right: technically, he was an end: no one can go further along his path. But thematically, he is the beginning. His great theme—and it is *his* great theme because despite its Nietzschean ancestry, no one had ever voiced it in fiction—is the abiding psychological tension of our modern world.

Kafka knows just how *exhausting* modernity and liberalism are, how pointless our individualism can feel. His works are filled with tempting images of the Old Ways: fathers, courts, castles, emperors, the timeless Law. His prose enshrines the temptation. It slides into something very like poetry as he describes the glory of belonging to a united people in "The Great Wall of China." In the *The Trial*, after all the hopelessness of legal argument, after dwelling so long with Josef K.'s deluded, lonely, modern soul, it feels like daylight when Kafka's language soars at last to describe the dying man's vision of the gleam that bursts inextinguishably from the Door to the Law.*

Kafka knows the deep, dark attraction of a backflip of faith that will take us again into the arms of supposedly eternal values. He knows that we miss the eagles and the trumpets, the certainties and the myths, the warmth of unquestioned, unquestioning *belonging*. We can all easily find ourselves longing for a simpler world where we don't have to worry about why the priest is stroking the choir-boy's head, or whether our rulers are legitimate, or our laws just. The liberal, rational "scientific traveller" of "In the Penal Colony" knows damn well that things are wrong here but he dreads the responsibility that would come with action and flees the White Liberal's Burden when it falls to him anyway. And even he cannot help but feel "the might of olden times."

Kafka's works are soaked in all the exhaustions of modern, secular man and all the temptations to retreat. He takes us so far with his deluded heroes that we all but accept their delusions. We find ourselves, too, longing for the code to the Door to the Law, for the Absolute Acquittal, the pass to the Castle, the Father's approval, the Emperor's Message . . .

---

* Kafka's German's extraordinary power comes from the underlying feeling that here is a could-be poet holding himself permanently in check—a thoroughly modern man who could, at any moment, let go and start writing like the Bible or Goethe (or perhaps, Stefan George). This is by its nature utterly impossible to prove, let alone translate.

But Kafka sees the world too clearly to fall for it. He knows that the supposedly timeless powers that be—like the hallowed Habsburg emperor whose law-abiding subject he was from his birth until he was thirty-five—actually depend on lies, illusions, and our sheer fear. They are all petty bureaucratic versions of Dostoyevsky's Grand Inquisitor: their words are grand and their claims are eternal but their robes are borrowed, their dirty underwear shows, their porn lies openly about in their courts and their public ceremonies of justice incarnate have decayed into creaking rites of murder. With God dead and buried (Kafka openly uses this arch-Nietzschean image in the cathedral scene of *The Trial*), it's all just about one thing: earthly power.

In an age when men yield themselves (and others) up to visions of the fountains of paradise, described in timeless glory down scrambled cell phones, Kafka's black-comic tales of what happens to modern people who can't give up on the Old Ways could hardly be more timely. He knows better than anyone that we all feel such yearnings, but he also knows that giving into them is a certain way to waste your life.

Saintly? No, Kafka was far more interesting than that. That's why we still read his books. That's why we always will. That's why we should be doing so now more than ever.

NOTES

I: The Way Things Were

1. *Diary*, 1 October 1911.
2. Brod, p. 137 and *Diary*, 3 November 1915. His view of the eastern Jews as "African" or "Asian"—they were, of course, nothing of the sort, all having come on trains from thoroughly European and Christian regions—was extremely common at the time. It was to become one of the psychological mainsprings of the Holocaust. But we'll see later the dangers of any sentence that includes the phrase, or even the idea, "was to become."
3. He's reading the almanac right around this time. See Alt, 433.
4. In the most detailed study of the family's factory, Anthony Northey decides that the picture of our hero as a merely theoretical asbestos-manufacturer (befitting an Almost Saintly Genius) is false: he "was one of the prime movers in the undertaking."
5. *Diary*, 2 October 1911 and letter to Felice, 18 November 1912.
6. One of his earliest, undated diary entries, sometime between May and November 1909, and entry for 19 December 1913.
7. Else Lasker-Schüler. See letter to Felice, 12 February 1913, and Stach, 213.
8. Recalls Brod.
9. This interpretation of events was very kindly given me in a private letter by Professor Peter-André Alt of Berlin, our hero's greatest biographer.

II: Into the Locked Bookcase

1. Sir Macolm Pasley preferred *The Transformation*. We might even go for *The Change* to bring out the comedy. But that discussion is for another day.

2. *The Observer* (London), May 17, 1998.

3. Alt, 138.

4. See Alt, 241.

III: Myth-making at Work

1. I've used the striking title Max Brod gave this novel and by which it's generally known. Kafka himself called it *Der Verschollene*, which is very hard to translate. *The Man Who Disappeared* seems rather clumsy, though correct. *The Man Who Went West?* Or even *Gone West?*

2. Alt, 184.

3. See Alt, 297.

4. Whatever else it did in its vile history, the Red Army shut down Auschwitz. Anyone who has forgotten how the Russians were received should read Primo Levi's accounts.

5. Said Elie Wiesel to me in 1998 when I interviewed him in Boston for the BBC.

6. For example, Irish census results are always disfigured by anyone who ever passed an exam in Gaelic claiming fluency in it. These people genuinely *wish* it were true, however, meaning that the political battle has been won.

7. Dora Diamant, quoted in Alt, 679.

IV: The Stages of the Myth

1. Simon Schama has recently debunked this myth concerning the other great contemporary contender, Van Gogh.

2. Ritchie Robertson, review of Peter-André Alts *Der ewige Sohn* in Zeitschrift für Germanistik 2/2006).

V: Kafka and Felice: Nothing to Do with Sex

1. Alt, 287; Robertson, *Brief Introduction*, 14.

2. For example, 11 November and 14 November 1911.

3. Alt, 82.

4. Letter of uncertain date, October/November 1914.

VI: Kafka and Milena: All About Sex

1. Milena to Brod, August 1920.

2. On November 24, 1912 he writes to Felice that "freeing himself" by writing the "disgusting story" (*The Metamorphosis*)—thereby, perhaps making himself "purer and more worthy" for her in the future—is "the most lustful business."

3. Milena to Brod, August 1920.

4. See Alt, 184.

5. This term is Elizabeth Boa's.

6. This insight is Angela Carter's in *The Sadeian Woman*.

VII: Why the Myth Must Go

1. Ritchie Robertson, *Kafka: Judaism, Literature and Politics*, 25.

2. Hans-Heiner Kühne, *Straf-Prozesslehre*, Heidelberg 1988, 2–3.

3. The German word *Rechtsstaat* doesn't mean the same thing. Nothing in English expresses the idea. *Constitutional state* might be close, but no human would ever say it, and any translation that sounds like something no one would ever say is by definition wrong.

4. *The Independent* (London), October 29, 1990.

FURTHER READING

This is easier than it sounds, because there are "no more than three or four introductions to Kafka published anywhere in the world that are worth reading" (Reiner Stach).

The most common English-language biographies are by Ronald Hayman and Ernst Pawel, both from the 1980s. Hayman is plodding, sometimes little more than a list of biographical events and never free of adulation. Pawel is much better: he's excellent on the historical milieu, only (but greatly) marred by doom-laden "little did they know"–style comments about the Holocaust on almost every other page. Nicholas Murray's recent biography is not well written and frankly doesn't add much.

The latest work now coming out of Germany changes everything. Reiner Stach's *Kafka: The Decisive Years* is the first volume of what will be a vast trilogy. It would be the standard work except that we have Peter André-Alt's huge, matchless, German prize-winning *Der ewige Sohn*, which beats it for imaginative boldness and analytic depth. In a fair if ruthless world, Stach would be like the brilliant tennis player who has the misfortune to play Wimbledon in the same years as Federer. But publishing isn't like that and Stach has the priceless advantage over Alt in that he's been translated into English.

In this language, Ritchie Robertson's *Kafka: A Very Brief Introduction* can't be beat. It's totally accessible, truly portable, and very attractively laid out. Also highly affordable, this little book is the equivalent of a stunning lecture series that doesn't overwhelm you with facts or jargon but leaves you wanting to rush to the nearest library and read more for yourself. With its excellent bibliography, there's really no better place to start—and Robertson's *Kafka: Judaism, Politics, and Literature* is a very good place to go next.

Otherwise, anything that Googles when you put Robertson's name together with Kafka's is worth reading, as is anything that comes up when you put in Sir Malcolm Pasley.

As for basic materials, Klaus Wagenbach's irresistibly illustrated books are deserved best sellers and Jürgen Born's work on Kafka's critical reception in his own day is absolutely necessary stuff.

You don't need any more than this, for the brutal fact is that there really is very little else that would be missed.

INDEX

Ackroyd, Peter, 139, 227–28
Almost Dying Kafka picture, 1, 75
Alt, Peter-André, 57, 81, 147–48, 190
Amerika (Kafka), 80, 125, 167, 205, 219
The Amethyst journal, 33, 200, 202
banning of, 60
Blei as publisher of, 60
pornography in, 60–69
Anecdotes (Kleist), 125
anti-Semitism, 97, 101
of Hitler, 89
in Prague, 103–4
Arcadia yearbook, 39
Brod as editor of, 47
Arkadia yearbook, 44
Austria, 27, 93, 98

Battle of Tagliamento, 95
Bauer, Felice (Kafka, F., fiancée), 30–32, 31, 34–35, 39, 48, 55, 94, 109–10, 116, 120, 129, 132, 140, 147, 149–50, 156–81, 189, 191–92, 200–201, 206, 209–11, 223

Bloch and, 150, 180, 191
Brod introduction of Kafka, F., to, 132, 156
Kafka, F., description of, 158, 179–80
Kafka, F., letter to, 94, 109, 120, 159–64, 160
Kafka, F., marriage proposal to, 110, 169–73
Kafka, F., prenuptial agreement and, 171
Kafka, F., relationship with, 147–48
Kafka, F., unsent letter to, 164–65
"Before the Law" (Kafka), 45, 108
Berlin Gay Museum, 58
Beyle, Marie-Henri. *See* Stendhal
Bleak House (Dickens), 192, 218–20, 227–29
Blei, Franz, 45, 55, 68, 115
as *Amethyst* publisher, 60
as Fontane Prize judge, 38–39
as *Hyperion* editor, 36, 38–39
as *Opals* publisher, 60
pornography of, 60–61

Index

Bloch, Grete (Felice's best friend)
  Kafka, F., affair with, 150, 180, 191
Bodleian Library, in Oxford University
  Kafka, F., porn in, 58
Bohemia newspaper, 22, 39
Bonaparte, Napoleon, 26–27, 167, 208
Bonaparte's Grande Armée, 26
Borchardt, Rudolf, 94
Brecht, Bertolt, 139, 229
British Library, Kafka porn in, 58
Brod, Max (Kafka's best friend), 36, 47,
  58, 59, 69, 77, 79, 86*n*, 103, 115,
  154, 161, 166, 186, 200, 216
  as *Arcadia* yearbook editor, 47
  as head of "Prague Circle" of writers,
    71
  "The Judgment" publication by,
    38–39
  Kafka, F., introduction to Felice by,
    132, 156
  Kafka, F., will and, 115–18
  porn of, 60–61
brothel/bordello, Kafka and, 32–33,
  59, 70, 83, 137, 186, 191, 200

Café Corso, 80, 151
The Castle (Kafka), 59, 80, 121, 124,
  142, 143, 186, 200, 211, 219,
  229
de Cervantes, Miguel, 4–5
Chapman, Charlie, 75–76
Chekhov, Anton, 4
Conrad, Joseph, 3, 9, 225
"Consolation in Suffering" (Goethe),
  207
Conversations of the Courtesans (Lucian),
  68
"A Country Doctor" (Kafka), 57,
  112–13, 116, 185
Czech National Theater, 94
"A Czech Serving Girl (Brod), 61, 79

The Dark Path (Blei), 38
The Day of Judgment publication
  of Wolff & Co., 38, 45
"Death of God" (Nietzsche), 122
"Description of a Struggle" (Kafka), 64

Diaries, Brod edition of, 69
diary, of Kafka, F., 26, 61, 80, 84–86,
  110, 128–29, 138, 142, 153,
  175–77, 186, 195, 206, 211, 224
Dickens, Charles, 4, 8, 124, 125, 139,
  192, 206, 218–20, 225, 227–29
Don Quixote (Cervantes), 4
Door to the Law, 4, 231
Dostoyevsky, Fyodor, 3, 124, 125, 225,
  228–29
Dr. Jackdaw, 78
  Kafka, F., as, 77

Eduardova, Yevgenya (dancer), 85, 87
  Kafka, F., and, 84–88
  as Riefenstahl's teacher, 88
Ehrenstein, Albert, 47, 115
Expressionist Generation, 121, 133

Faust (Goethe), 86, 154, 205, 207
Felice. *See* Bauer, Felice
Fischer of Berlin publishing company,
  37
Fischer, Samuel
  as *New Review* publisher, 37–38
Flaubert, Gustave, 3, 4, 31, 228
Fletcher, Horace, 24
Fletcherizing, 24
The Fly (Poe), 6
Fontane Prize, 38, 60, 112
  Blei as judge of, 38–39
  Kafka, F., award of, 40–48, 54, 71,
    108
  Sternheim as 1915 winner of, 39,
    46
Frankenstein sanatorium
  Kafka, F., and, 91–96
  for war-damaged mental patients, 91
Franz Kafka: Eine Chronik (Wagenbach),
  59, 107
Freud, Sigmund, 16–17, 84, 206, 220

Gallipoli debacle, 14, 19
George, Stefan, 57–58
German-Bohemians, 97
  folk-comrades of, 23, 92, 95, 97
  of Prague, 22

Index

Germany
  Jews in, 89–90, 98, 101
  law of, 213–15
  Middle Europe capture by, 20
  Nazification of, 89–90
  Schlieffen Plan, 17
von Goethe, Johann Wolfgang, 4, 86,
    90, 99, 125, 154, 205, 208, 223
  Kafka, F., influenced by, 206–7,
    210
government bonds, 15, 15–16, 71,
    111, 191
  of Habsburg Empire, 14
  Kafka, F., purchase of, 26–27, 49–50
Grand Inquisitor (Dostoyevsky), 232
"The Great Wall of China" (Kafka),
    110, 121, 142, 231
Great War, 13, 16–21, 27, 89–90, 95,
    98–99, 103, 111–12, 138, 141,
    156, 215
The Great Year 1914–1915 (Fischer), 26

Habsburg Empire, 21, 79–80, 88, 91,
    92, 98, 102, 215, 232
  Austria of, 93
  government bonds of, 14
  Josef of, 13–15
  purpose of, 218–20
Hamlet (Shakespeare), 8, 209, 212
Hegel, Georg Wilhelm Friedrich, 21,
    179
Hesse, Hermann, 115
Hesse, Otto, 126
Hitler, Adolf, 88, 89–90, 114, 133–34,
    139
  anti-Semitism of, 89
Holmes, Sherlock, 223, 225–26, 230
  Kafka, F., observational method
    from, 8
Holocaust, 5, 97, 102, 206, 211, 223
  Kafka, F., and, 88–91
Holy Hairbrush, of Kafka, 56
"A Hunger Artist" (Kafka), 114, 116,
    208
Hunger Artist Notebook, 143
Hyperion journal
  Blei, as editor of, 36, 38–39

"In the Penal Colony" (Kafka), 49,
    109–10, 116, 126, 231
International Zionist Congress (1913),
    99
"Investigations of a Dog" (Kafka), 208

"Jackals and Arabs" (Kafka), 109
Jacob, Heinrich Eduard, 47
James, Henry, 3, 163
Jews, 6, 97–99
  in Austria, 98
  in Germany, 89–90, 98, 101
  Kafka, F., as, 8, 23, 96, 103, 119–26
  Kafka, H., as Tough, 121–22
  in Prague, 100–104, 124
Josef, Franz, 13–15, 17, 98–99, 215
"Josefine the Singer" (Kafka), 86, 97
Joyce, James, 3, 4, 8, 9, 198, 202, 209
"The Judgment" (Kafka), 108, 116,
    136, 147, 152, 159, 163, 177,
    192, 210, 216
  Brod publication of, 38–39
  story of, 223–25
Julie. *See* Wohryzeck, Julie
Jungborn Sanatorium, 41, 154, 155,
    207

Kafka: A Biography of His Youth
    (Wagenbach), 58
Kafka, Bruno, 95
Kafka, Franz, 8, 28–30, 30, 32, 49, 53,
    57, 61, 64, 70, 80, 86, 97, 108
  as asbestos manufacturer, 31, 35, 50,
    138, 161, 192
  bachelorhood of, 32–35, 149–52
  bizarre world of, 211–20
  brothel/bordello and, 32–33, 59, 70,
    83, 137, 186, 191, 200
  as Czech, 29, 100
  death of, 114–15
  diary of, 26, 61, 80, 84–86, 110,
    128–29, 138, 142, 153, 175–77,
    186, 195, 206, 211, 224
  diet of, 24, 141, 175
  dog in picture with, 81–82
  as Dr. Jackdaw, 77
  Eduardova and, 84–88

Kafka, Franz (*continued*)
Felice, fiancée of, 30–32, *31,* 34–35,
  39, 48, 55, 94, 109–10, 116, 120,
  129, 132, 140, 147, 149–50,
  156–81, 191–92, 200–201, 206,
  209–11, 223
first sexual encounter of, 193,
  196–98
Fontane Prize award to, 40–48, 54,
  71, 108
Frankenstein sanatorium and, 91–96
Goethe influence on, 206–7, 210
government bonds purchased by,
  26–27, 49–50
health of, 122–23, 165–66, 169,
  171
Hitler and, 83–88
Holocaust and, 88–91
Holy Hairbrush of, 56
as insurance expert, 22–29
as investor, 14–16, 26–27, 49–50,
  71
as Jew, 8, 23, 96, 103, 119–26
Julie, as third fiancée of, 116, 129,
  136, 157, 189, 199, 200
K.-myths of, 5–7, 9, 54–55, 57,
  70–71, 93–94, 104, 107–40, 177,
  225
as lawyer, 22, 41, 118, 175
Milena and, 94, 104, 116, 125, 129,
  135, 137–38, 141, 185–202, *188,*
  192, 194, 211
Oxford University collection of, 55
picture of, *1, 24,* 27, *30*
porn of, 9, 57–60, 137, 186, 191,
  196, 223
prostitutes and, 61, 69–70, 196–98,
  200
servicemen, mentally damaged and,
  91–96
sex and, 185–202
Spanish flu of, 111, 141
Szokoll as sexual playmate of, 77,
  80–83, 199, 201
TB illness and, 111, 127–28,
  140–43, 192
wealth of, 110–11, 128

wills of, 115–18
Wolff & Co., 38–41, 45, 108, 112,
  114, 118, 168
Wolff and, 37, 40, 108–9, 113, 154
as writer, 36–40, 108–14, 229–30
Zionism of, 120
Zürau Aphorism of, 199
Kafka, Hermann, 65, 128, *135,* 192,
  200, 210, 211
Kafka, F., letter to, 133, 135, 136,
  139
as liberal father, 137–40
as monstrous, 130–40
as Tough Jew, 121–22
Kaiser-Battle, of Great War, 111
Keats, John, 4, 60, 206
von Kleist, Heinrich, 117, 125
Klimt, Gustav, erotic illustrations of,
  69, 79, 80
K.-myth, 5, 9, 54–55, 57, 70–71,
  93–94, 104, 177, 225
"facts" of, 6–7
Kafka, F., as poor/lonely, 127–30
Kafka, F., as unknown, 107–15
Kafka, F., crippling TB, 140–43
Kafka, F., father as monstrous,
  130–40
Kafka, F., Jewishness, 119–26
Kafka, F., mysterious/opaque style,
  126–27
Kafka, F., works destroyed after
  death, 115–19
The Knickers (Sternheim), 39
Kurt Wolff & Co. *See* Wolff & Co.

"Letter to His Father" (Kafka), 133,
  135, 139, 195

Malte Laurids Brigge (Rilke), 127
Meditation (Kafka), 37, 44, 108, 116,
  158
Mein System (Müller), *25,* 122–23
The Metamorphosis (Kafka), 44, 80, 108,
  109, 114, 116, 120, 124, 126,
  161, 167, 180, 210, 227
about man turning into beetle, 53,
  205, 207–9

The Metamorphosis Back of Gregor Samsa
(Kafka), 108
Meyer, G. H., 40–43, 45
Milena. *See* Pollack, Milena
Mirbeau, Octave, 67, 68
Miss Falcon, 78
Szokoll as, 77
Mitteleuropa, *19,* 96
Great War end and, 111–12
Mona Lisa, 55
Müller, J. P., 25, 122–23
Müllerizing, 25, 175–76, 179
Munn, Thomas, 178
Murray, Nicholas, 89
Musil, Robert
as *New Review* editor, 37–38, 45, 115
Mussolini, Benito, 94, 134

Napoleon (Sternheim), 43–45
The National News, 47
New Free Press, 47
New Review, 114, 126, 180
Fischer as publisher of, 37–38
Musil as editor of, 37–38, 45, 115
Nietzsche, 8, 35, 86, 122, 123, 133,
220, 230
Nuremberg Laws, 89

Opals journal, 33
Blei as publisher of, 60
pornography in, 60–69
Oxford University, Kafka collection at,
55

Pasley, Malcolm, 55, 82
Pawel, Ernst, 54, 61, 101
Penthouse, 61–62
Petersburg Ballet, 86
Poe, Edgar Allan, 6
Pollack, Ernst, 188
Pollack, Milena, 116, 125, 129, 135,
137–38, 141, *188,* 211
Kafka, F., letter to, 94, 104, 192,
194
Kafka, F., relationship with,
185–202
as Kafka, F., translator, 188–89

pornography (porn), *62, 63, 64, 66, 67,*
68
in *Amethyst/Opals* journal, 60–69
of Blei/Brod, 60–61
of Kafka, F., 9, 57–60, 137, 186,
191, 196, 223
of Kafka, F., in Bordleian/British
library, 58
Prague, 13
anti-semitism, 103–4
German working class in, 79
German-Bohemians of, 22
Jews in, 100–104, 124
"party girls" in, 78–79
sexual imperialism in, 80
waitress, *33*
"Prague Circle" of writers
Brod as head of, 71
Prague Daily News, 13–14, 20, 22, 47,
80, 102, 108
Prophetic Kafka, 5
prostitutes
Kafka, F., and, 61, 69–70, 196–98,
200
Proust, Marcel, 3, 4
Punishment (Kafka), 44

"Reasonable Force" (Brod), 216
Red Army, 89–90
"The Refusal" (Kafka), 64–65,
150–51
"A Report for an Academy" (Kafka),
109, 185
Reuss, Roland, 117–18
Revelations of a Chambermaid (Mirbeau),
67
Riefenstahl, Leni
Eduardova as teacher of, 88
Hitler and, 88
Rilke, Rainer Maria, 36, 109, 115, 127
Robertson, Ritchie, 148
Rockefeller, J. P., 24
La Ronde (Reigen) (Schnitzler), 79,
198
Russia, 17, 95
prisoners from, 20
Red Army of, 89–90

Sacher-Masoch (Baron), 68, 81
Saintly Che Guevara, 5
Schlieffen Plan, of Germany, 17
Schnitzler, Arthur, 42–43, 65, 98, 138, 198
Sentimental Education (Flaubert), 125
Shakespeare, William, 3, 4, 8, 55, 206, 209, 212
Sin and Other Stories (Mirbeau), 67
Smiling Kafka in a Bowler Hat picture, 75, 76
The Sorrows of Young Werther (Goethe), 208
Spanish flu, of Kafka, F., 111, 141
Stach, Reiner, 93
Stalin, Josef, 89–90
Steiner, Marianne, 55
Steiner, Rudolf, 23
Stendhal (Beyle, Marie-Henri), 3, 228
Sternheim, Carl (playwright), 41, 43–45, 115
    as 1915 Fontane Prize winner, 39, 46
The Stoker (Kafka), 108, 109, 170
Szokoll, Hansi, as Kafka, F.'s, sexual playmate, 80–83, 199, 201
    dog in picture with, 81–82
    as Miss Falcon, 77

TB. *See* tuberculosis
Torture Garden (Mirbeau), 68
de Toulouse-Lautrec, Henri, 79
Translations (Friel), 218
The Trial (Kafka), 70, 80, 82, 118–19, 124, 126, 129, 152, 185–86, 211–12, 214–15, 219–20, 225, 228–29, 231–32
Triumph of the Will (movie)
    Riefenstahl in, 88
Trocadero, 69, 80, 151, 199, 200

tuberculosis (TB), 192
    of Kafka, F., 111, 127–28, 140–43
"Turned Down" (Kafka), 185

Ulysses (Joyce), 8, 9, 209

Venus in Furs (Sacher-Masoch), 68, 81–82
Viennese Imperial Opera, 95
Volksgenossen (folk-comrades), 23, 92, 95, 97

Wagenbach, Klaus, 59, 107
    as Kafka, F., collector/publisher, 5
Wannsee Conference, 89–90
"The War and the German Decision" (Borchardt), 94
"Wedding Preparations in the Country" (Kafka), 65
Weiler, Hedwig, 195
Weiss, Ernst, 47, 115
Werfel, Franz, 28, 115, 125, 157, 187
The Whim of Eros (Brod), 60–61
White Pages journal
    Wolff & Co. publication of, 38
Wilhelm (Kaiser), 17–18, 22
Wohryzeck, Julie, 116, 129, 189, 199, 200
    Kafka, F., father's scorn of, 136
    as Kafka, F., third fiancée, 136, 157
Wolff & Co., 37–41, 45, 108, 112, 114, 118, 168
    The Day of Judgment publication by, 38, 45
    White Pages publication by, 38
Wolff, Kurt, 37, 40, 108–9, 113, 154.
    See also Wolff & Co.
World War I. *See* Great War

Zionists, 99, 120
Zürau Aphorisms, of Kafka, F., 199